THE PUZZLE

other books by the author

POETRY
Dawn Visions
Burnt Heart/Ode to the War Dead
This Body of Black Light Gone Through the Diamond
The Desert is the Only Way Out
The Chronicles of Akhira
The Blind Beekeeper
Mars & Beyond
Laughing Buddha Weeping Sufi
Salt Prayers
Ramadan Sonnets
Psalms for the Brokenhearted
I Imagine a Lion
Coattails of the Saint
Abdallah Jones and the Disappearing-Dust Caper
Love is a Letter Burning in a High Wind
The Flame of Transformation Turns to Light
Underwater Galaxies
The Music Space
Cooked Oranges
Through Rose Colored Glasses
Like When You Wave at a Train and the Train Hoots Back at You
In the Realm of Neither
The Fire Eater's Lunchbreak
Millennial Prognostications
You Open a Door and it's a Starry Night
Where Death Goes
Shaking the Quicksilver Pool
The Perfect Orchestra
Sparrow on the Prophet's Tomb
A Maddening Disregard for the Passage of Time
Stretched Out on Amethysts
Invention of the Wheel
Sparks Off the Main Strike
Chants for the Beauty Feast
In Constant Incandescence
Holiday from the Perfect Crime
The Caged Bear Spies the Angel
The Puzzle

THEATER / THE FLOATING LOTUS MAGIC OPERA COMPANY
The Walls Are Running Blood
Bliss Apocalypse

PROSE
Zen Rock Gardening
The Little Book of Zen
Zen Wisdom

THE PUZZLE

POEMS

March 21, 1992 – August 17, 1993

Daniel Abdal-Hayy Moore

The Ecstatic Exchange
2011
Philadelphia

The Puzzle
Copyright © 2011 Daniel Abdal-Hayy Moore
All rights reserved.
Printed in the United States of America

For quotes any longer than those for critical articles and reviews, contact:
The Ecstatic Exchange,
6470 Morris Park Road, Philadelphia, PA 19151-2403
email: abdalhayy@danielmoorepoetry.com

First Edition
ISBN: 978-0-578-08891-4
Published by *The Ecstatic Exchange*,
6470 Morris Park Road, Philadelphia, PA 19151-2403

Also available from The Ecstatic Exchange:
Knocking from Inside, poems by Tiel Aisha Ansari

Acknowledgments: Some of these poems (*Dust*, etc.) were originally published in *Ecstasis*, a journal edited by Geoffrey Manaugh.

Cover collage, title page drawing, lithograph of Arthur Rimbaud page 61, sketch page 211 by the author
Back cover photograph by Malika Moore

DEDICATION

To
Shaykh ibn al-Habib (Allah be pleased)
(and the continuation of the Habibiyya)
Shaykh Bawa Muhaiyuddeen,
all shuyukh of instruction and ma'arifa
my wife Malika
(teacher of generosity and kindness)
and family,

and
Baji Tayyaba Khanum
of the unsounded depths

---

*The earth is not bereft
of Light*

CONTENTS

The Puzzle   9
Aphorisms   15
Canyons   17
Certain Poets   18
In a World   20
Poem with Two Characters from Shakespeare   22
Unrequited Love   24
Dust   26
Point of Departure   30
Whitman's Deathbed   36
Some Poems I Would Like to Write   39
When I Get Transformed into a Woman   45
Be in a Foreign Country   50
The Man from Porlock   52
Sleep and Waking   55
Middle of the Night   58
Rimbaud in Aden   60
Reading Oneself   62
Body-Lock   64
Stripes   66
Rock   71
Atlantic City Nature Poem   73
Annunciatory Angel   77
Small Enigmatic Poem   79
Airline Flight 774   80
Avalanche   82
Death   84
Further Aphorisms   86
On Being a Guest at Puzzle Castle   89

St. Sebastian and St. Jerome's Lion   95
Toes   97
On Being a Guest at Puzzle Castle II   98
Diversionary Interlude from Puzzle Castle   100
Train   105
Sleep Twist   110
To be Completely Open   111
Used Bookstore Owner   113
The Puzzle at Present   115
Getting Dressed   134
Life and Death   136
In Memoriam David Rattray 1937-1993   148
Another Day   150
Full Moon   158
Baseball Stadium Epiphany   162
I Am a Stubborn Man   163
The Poet Dies   164
Back Stairs   167
The Wait   168
Puzzlements   173
The New Town   175
The Act of Love   177
Mockingbird   179
After the End of the World   186
The Puzzle Potentized   189

INDEX   212

I am exposed... cut by bitter and poisoned hail,
Steeped amid honeyed morphine... my windpipe squeezed in
    the fakes of death,
Let up again to feel the puzzle of puzzles,
And that we call Being.

— Walt Whitman, *Song of Myself (line 607)*

When those who love God try to talk about Him
their words are blind lions looking for springs
in the desert.

— Leon Bloy

THE PUZZLE

1
for Malika

I sit in a Chinese labyrinth
   just off the main hall, for I can hear
     elegant conversation within.
Teak polished to mirror smoothness shows me myself
  as a man with a ladder face
    on a plumaged neck of grouse or
      ruffed pheasant. Hands like jade
tongs. It's an
  astonishing transformation, and only because
I couldn't answer the supreme puzzle.

I was given objects in blocks of amber to identify,
pearls on invisible strings, fossils in glass,
drawings viewed only from behind,
   maps to territories with
     interplanetary names, like
    Pollen Dust in Space, Float of Gymnosperm,
      Ariadne's Petit Point.

I washed in seven sacred seas the color of blood.
I let my face re-emerge on the surface like an
     orange bathed in blue moonlight.
The bandits were beheaded as I counted the emperor's take
   from unjust taxation.
I ate only prawns dipped in Mongolian opium.

But the spindly tree in the courtyard knows the answer to the puzzle.
Yesterday winter snow followed by sleet
    turned it into a tall bundle of
glass rods and crystal twigs, perfectly transparent, glittering
      like sparklers.
Buds already unfurl at the tips of its branches.
Pinwheels of golden flowers soon will appear
    spinning among its limbs.
      Summer will see it a dense parasol full of
        birds hunting inchworms, alert and
  nimble as light.

The tree doesn't speak to passersby, only to stones.

Stones gather around its
base to hear its parables.

I've overheard the end of a phrase, and then been found out.
They all fell silent until I left.

So, how do I know the tree has uncovered the conundrum?

It changes and never changes.
It sways but isn't blown down.
It refuses to be less than it is, even
    stripped bare.

Sunlight loves its leaves.

It speaks into the wind.

2

How was I to know that between
   one elegant metaphor and the next
      bellied an abyss of improbability so
large bus loads of obese theologians from the low countries
         could be driven
      into it for weeks on end?

How was I to know that the tax money of the
   upper crust would be paraded
      before me dressed in tiny costumes of rags and
cloaks with ripped pouches, coins on
crutches and bank notes on stretchers with
fresh slobber on their little green chins?

How was I, a mere court functionary, whose
mother wore hip boots of native rubber and whose
   father called animals with the shape of his
         mouth, whose
      ancestors glanced
         sideways at clouds and knew the
            exact day's curve of
               temperature,

suddenly confronted with the puzzle running vertically rather than
half-submerged and half-emerged on the
   horizontal, be expected, in elaborately artificial court
language, to know its answer?

I had been brought up on a daily ration of

    small miracles, it's true,
and was present when the
waterfall on north corner turned to cold jade and
        stopped its watery motion,
but to be prepared for the puzzle was
another thing altogether, not some
plaything of children under holiday tables.

Deception plays such a large part in our daily experience,
from the bird food that insists on looking like
     dead leaves, then
        flutters away when the
          bird's not looking, to
our own thoughts about our own selves
slapping coat after coat of neon paint over a
     sore point until it
       blinks and glares so
   brightly no one, least of all ourselves, can
     bear to look
         straight at it.

It took the sickness that kept me under blankets of
gold leaf and mortal terror,
the death of the old garage mechanic who used to
       fix the Prince's
         mechanical roosters,
and reaching an age where certain sexual signs
      could be read between the
        haphazard fall of the
          soothsayer's bones on the
      bald parquet.

Then I couldn't tell you the answer to the puzzle in so many
words, but I could
stand by the pillar in such a way that
    some of the afternoon light would
        reflect off your sleeve as well,
or cup water from the cold stream for
your mouth as well as my own.
Then radiators in the depths of night might not
boil over with such regularity,
and staircases built against blank walls with no
    doors in them
might not fool anyone less than 90 years old
holding onto the glass key that breaks in
all locks but one,

the ubiquitous heart come alive at the
sound of daybreak, breathing deeply of the
first element to make its
    daily appearance, and
drinking in influences from beyond the dragon screen of
secondary illusions.

When I reached the court I remembered what my
grandmother had instructed me:
Learn correct pronunciation;
  give back exact change;
never walk ahead of those with
    greater knowledge than yourself — but
separate the silk from the silkiness,
water from wetness,
  the dark saying from the

bright inner meaning.

She never died. She merely
    expired into a
      subtlety.

How was I to know
breath was mathematical,
   doilied at the end with
     filagreed lace so fine
       it melts imperceptibly into the
five elements?

How was I to know the
owl of blind truth would perch on my
   branch and look out these
mortal eyes at a
     world forever melting?

                                                               3/21

APHORISMS

"A serpent won't stay long in oiled hands."
"No reply from a virgin means 'yes,' no
  reply from a tyrant means war."
"If a horse is saddled in silver
    ride it regally."
"A hollow room in a house is
      friendlessness."
"Know the seasons as you know the back of your
  hand: both inevitably come to an end."

Tablets of teak against teak doorjambs, incised in
    occult alphabets. Letters eaten out of the
        wood by worms.
The Great Eastern Hall was filled with these worm-scribbled texts.
Thousands of aphorisms by the late mad
    emperor who made
      every occasion an occasion for
        paradox.
Some recalled ancient adages:
  "One hair on a crane is like a moth
    in fancy armor."
  "A knife of light drawn against smoke
    dispels wrong actions."
  "One mountain is enough on a horizon of
    small hills."
Others paid homage to our
  irrational natures:
  "A star seen by a bat is not part of the
    nightingale's heaven."

"Elephant trees move slowly across the attentive mind."
"Lady Pin's fan engenders silken sashes."

Moonlight bathes the blind surfaces of these
    tablets as they face
        the direction of the
Great Western Hall, toward the
      heavenly volcano

of the Great Western Hall.

CANYONS

A silken development soon enveloped us
   after the ignition required occurred.
Several elegant angles accommodated, several
      grooves. You said,
"The music sounds like canyons," and into
   canyons we flowed.
This is lovemaking at its best, *de rigueur* for the species,
    definite as
       glass, intrigued by the
          possibilities. All the pods.
Burst into a million green filaments.
Feathery pollen-rods, feathery and antenna-like, searching
    a way.
  Ripple incessantly. Draw in the
     sea. Foam of

     formations.

CERTAIN POETS

When certain poets open their mouths
   a thousand ships fitted for commerce
      set out on impossible voyages —
ship silhouettes float on fiery horizons like the recently drowned.
They may come back with precious prize or
   newly drawn maps, or we may just hear
the haunted creaking of rigging, ropes against wood,
     the low monotonous grumbling of crews, the slosh of
bilge in hundreds of swinging lifeboats.

When other poets open their mouths
dead branches fall through living ones in dense forests.
Small rays of light slant down onto matted needles.
Bugs and earthworms slip between
   leaves like shuttlecocks on huge looms making
      intricate tapestries
while birds as swift as scarlet threads
    loop through available openings in
       the dense green air.

Other poets open their mouths
and car wrecks make disastrous racket at congested intersections,
hundreds of victims slump over
   steering wheels, last visions
     imprinted forever on
    dry irises, last words
      unuttered forever on drawn
        lips.

Some poetry covers the entire display with white sheets.
Snow soon fills deep dips and frosts high peaks
    with glistening light.

We who live on earth
see only part of the earth.
We who live in the sky
see only its vast underbelly.

Inside mind's arena of cloud-visions
    small antelope seem to be making their
        lithe way through frothing white billows in the
surface of a still sea.
Small cries can be heard at heavily patrolled borders,
people in the shapes of
    high-strung guinea-hens and aggressive black geese

impatiently wait to

enter the forbidden zones.

                                                4/1

IN A WORLD

In a world where people dive down into the earth in death
as others burst up newborn as if thrust on springs,
but neither acknowledges the other in their
dark passage, we're all alone in our
      trajectory —

in a world where everything's on sale except the constituent
      atomic elements they're made of,
so that things treasured, prized, fought and
  killed over are made of one
    substance taking many shapes, and under the
intense heat of a nuclear sun they might all melt
  together and turn out to be
     identical, a diamond the size of
    Toledo the same thing as scrap iron from a railroad track or
    a brand new soup ladle.

In a world where sky and ocean are like two
    hands of one body rubbing constantly together,
      clasping and unclasping, vapors and
        clouds and sea-depths eternally
          interchanging,

in this world a blind singer stands up in an
automobile graveyard and opens his or her
arms and opens his or her
lips, and silken bands of renewal
loosen and tighten at the same time around
    essential substances. The

eyes of the sighted glisten with otherworldly light
and silence takes on a softer texture than the
    tight-lipped face of the guardian of our
        mortality would suggest.

                                                      4/3

POEM WITH TWO CHARACTERS FROM SHAKESPEARE

The sound of a horse going by in the street
inside a wooden box
brought me close to a certain century, or the
atmosphere of a century where
silver might tarnish more slowly, lute-music might
drift out of a dark doorway down a
    cobblestone street, eggs might
    roll along a windowsill, heavy sacks of
ingots might clang against rough harbor boards as
a one-eyed mendicant with a single bread-end
might scatter pigeons with one hand while a
skinny black cat steals the one bread-end out of his bag.

In that subtler century
music charted the air between us with its
tiny animated black notes on wavy horizontal staves
    zigzagging around corners, down
  stairways, out into the
     open air of a square where people like
Mercutio might get stabbed when a hot
  bird of irrational passion rose up in them willing to
    burn in the atomic conflagration of its most
      multi-colored Kodachrome feathers vividly
    opalescent and iridescently pheasant-like
or phoenix-like, so that when the smile of
play suddenly turns to the brown frown of tragedy and
    Mercutio's limp body is lifted away by his
pals, the giant shadow crossing the square might be of

Ophelia heading out to the middle of the
lacy cloud-pond of the sky, and the

clop of hooves that sounds now like the
flip of fish in a pond, the breezes like the
buzz of flies around reeds, the
softly singing blips and gurgles of
water around all floating objects as they
catch the last rays of the setting sun, these clopping hooves just
continue clopping down
   cobblestone streets,

these sounds of clopping hooves just continue
    clopping in the
wooden box of this century's
      revery.

4/4

UNREQUITED LOVE

A tiny square of light bright yellow
   across the valley shows me
she's home and in her room
dreaming elephant butterfly Mongolian possibilities
instead of me.

Her angular room full of huge metal furniture.
Slanted shadows from tables and bedsteads
flash along the wall. Pails of
milk, one inside the other, soft
galvanized tin so
alloyed you can't see your
face in it.

I urge my thoughts, urge and urge my
thoughts, urge my
thoughts out through space, urge my
thoughts in the night, urge and
urge them on quicksilver darts to
fly through her square window right now
and into her thought-stream.

There they go, like geese going south, some
leading others, out through the
night, slip inside her
window and into her
thought-stream so turbulent and
coiling with
ripples folded in ripples as huge as

the Amazon, Tigris, and the
great Mississip'
all rolled into one.

My escape speedboats of spectacular elopements, my
heartbeating house on a hill, my
caravan pack animals packed up with
rare spices and frail woven silks, my
elocution add-arrangement shell-dome
kleptomania in the person of a
shifty relative of mine, my
jewels as big as golf balls, all for
her who ignores me, whose name is
    Separation.

My thought of the big black cat with vacant
square centers for eyes, amber so
clear, teeth so sharp, claws so curved, heart so
beating, stomach so
hungry, eats her up, gulps her
down, she doesn't
scream, she slides right
in, it's my
love for her, my longing, the cat is better than
me in expressing it.
Now she's gone.

I'm all alone.

4/11

DUST

1

Everywhere dust is falling at the same rate.
It doesn't fall on the criminal any faster than
    on the saint.
It falls on the furniture and on our
feet about to enter our slippers after a short nap
as well as on the early colonist's graveyard down the street.
It falls, but we rarely see it fall.

In a barn on a Tuesday in the summer with
  a light ray falling all the way
    down from the hayloft window to our
feet we sometimes see the dancing particles falling,
tiny golden flakes of dust from some
upturned bin in heaven, or a crust of dust flaking off from a
    lower ozone layer in space.

Or maybe it's rising from down below our feet in a slow cosmic
    rotation, or is it

manufactured right out of nothingness so that all the
somethings in existence don't become too proud
to be above having a thin but gradually unmistakable
  patina of dust on them
    just for occupying space?

2

Dust in the mouth of Walt Whitman sleeping with his
   mouth open on the
100th anniversary of his death dreaming of being
    chased by a giant dust-mite
      down a crack in America the size of
        human greed.

Dust falling regularly on the sarcophagus at Cheops
    putting a fresh layer of living dust on
      a mummy who wishes he could
        just turn to dust and be gone.

Dust falling in pyramid-shaped flakes on
Chinese tractors, and in tractor-shaped flakes on
Egyptian pyramids.

Dust as old as Olduvai Gorge
   still swirling up and
     softly dropping down on new-born jawbones as well as
   missing-link jawbones getting their
trillionth layer of dust as they lie in the ancient sun waiting for an
archaeologist in fresh pressed khaki to
     uncover them and dust them off at last.
Living dust on
mantles and end-tables, new dust around the
mouths of politicians promising
   nothing that can hold up a
     ton or two of pure dust.

Dust into which we scramble down and lie flat as if playing dead
    when we die
and up from which we stand up full height at birth
dusting ourselves off and rolling up our
   sleeves and getting
right down to work, paid minimum wage 8 hours a day for
    pushing around various
      piles of pure dust.

Dust on distant mountaintops at dusk
  on which we sit down to contemplate
collecting on our heads some lovely particles of
     transcendental dust.

Oh, to enumerate everywhere dust collects would take
all day, and probably most of tomorrow!
And would we have
accomplished anything more than a
   more or less self-aware
outer skin of dust?

Dust of never being able to stop long enough to
enumerate all the things of this world which
    collect dust.

Dust so diffuse it falls even between
floating flakes of dustiest dust!

Do we see the tiny dust elves who scurry around under the
falling flakes away from prying eyes also made of
     genetic dust?

Or the dust-mite world, ferocious plated
    creatures gobbling and snorfling around in the
       dust, flinging
     it onto their backs the way elephants do
        with dirt to keep cool,
then rolling around in it again just for fun,
    then they can be seen
standing up on trembling legs, getting back to
    work, making their
      weary but happy way over ridges of
        dust to continue
doing whatever dust-mites do with dust.

O dust making all this possible!

Dear dust of infinite possibility.

Dear, dear dust impossible to
    ever be done with —

      Ever-popular dust!

4/16

POINT OF DEPARTURE

> *Set out from any point. They are all alike. They all lead to a point of departure.*
> — Antonio Porchia

1

Take as point of departure this
  oboe note like a crystal rosebud
blooming in the palm of your right hand held still for a
    micro-second in a straight ray of zonked blue sunlight.

Take this
point oriented east of north twenty degrees
as the hub of all earthly possibilities
from which anything occurs. Throaty and
deep undersea chords of a respectable
    death by drowning, coral crown built up to the
sunny surface replacing the top of your skull
    in a wavering mirror of dark currents
        coiling at the base of
            industrious continents.

This could be the stepping-off point for all of us,
the secret hatchway to generalized Ascension.

We might all take off at once into that sphere.

2

Or take as point of departure this
   single ant on the bathroom floor at my
      feet as I
         sit on the toilet amazed, this creature no
bigger than an
eyelash with legs goes
   lickety-split in one direction, stops, feels, turns
      180°, goes off in a new direction, stops, doubles
         back, goes straight, pauses,
resumes, stops and trundles back in the
   original direction again with intense dedication, and I

imagine a scum one or two molecules
   high this ant can see that I can't, the whole
      tile floor microscopically
         crisscrossed with interesting
trails to this ant, who makes
choices, decisions — I put my belt-tip near it,
it sniffs but doesn't climb, goes
   off in a new direction! Tiny tininess, eyes and
      feelers, feet going like crazy, perfectly
         normal for an ant,
and above it on the huge toilet a scanning
human looking down with eyeballs bigger than
it is, one foot-stamp and it's
gone, dear thing, which I
   do not do, it flashes through my mind, but I reject it.

Just as this oblivious creature never sees more of

me than a few edges, rejects one direction, one
   smell, one possible trail —
      goes off in another.

3

To take as point of departure
   anything or anywhere — what an idea!
We come into this world on a wave,
we go out on a wave, a big white ocean
   flows through the boundaries on either
      side, a bright green triangular moon at the close end,
a flashing blue sun at the far end with
bubbling black surf sizzling beneath it
as we let out a great whooping shout as we,
wildly waving, go out.

I mean, here I sit in space isolated in much the same way as
the ant in the second part of this poem, myself not much
   more than an eyelash with legs,
having come from somewhere — indecisively
      poised over a hologram of the
         Great Wall of China just below me
            beaming pale yellow light
         as it zigzags and snakes over those
            hills barren as iron from one
         bald Chinese province to another —
going somewhere, or nowhere,
   parasols of various heavens painted with
      various weathers overhead.

We jot down stars, we breathe the
silken threads of the
Milky Way of this galaxy —
do we hope for an Epiphany so great and
   vast, blasting us at once through so many
      dimensions of extraterrestrial rainbow overcoats that when we
come back we won't have to do the dishes ever again, or dust?

We come back, our frail arms and legs draped with
   the gangly crepe paper of Paradise, roll up our

sleeves and sink hairy arms up to their
   elbows in dishwater suds, drawing out
a tin plate so battered it won't ever reflect our
   face again, setting it on its side in the
sun so all those
   pearls of moisture will
      evaporate into pure air again.

Point of departure! Everything
   sinks back into the elements, drawn out and
   down great hallways to the
Source-shop of atomic formulations from
   seraphic stuff into hard matter,
angel fingertips wetted and drawn across each
   material surface to make it emit a
      celestial music as it
serves its perfectly practical purpose
wiling away its time down here
      on the whirling
         earth, our point of entrance, our

single point of departure.

4

Taking as point of departure
   the Great Wall of China, if you
      happen to be standing on it, in one of its
   guard towers, hearing the antique moans of one of the
men buried deep in its stones —

taking as point of departure one of the great
   historic moments, the founding of a
nation, men dressed in their
      best leaning over a charter with gold pens poised,
   eyes shining with as-yet-unrealized
      idealisms and as-yet-untarnished
         hopes, if you
   happen to be one of them, or one of the surrounding ones,
or even the servants waiting out in the hall —

taking as point of departure
the saint's armchair, the silken pillow used for his
   feet, or the windowsill upon which
  doves pecked the bread-crumbs he left for them each afternoon,
if you happen to be near him or near
     where he was not long after his
        point of departure —

Ah, taking as point of departure
any holy, antique, well-trod or even

    virgin path or place,
        situation, holy or unholy, ancient or
new, hallowed or unhallowed by being
thought of by us as a point of departure, exactly
where we are now, since every
  nook of space and cranny of time is
    packed with angels, luminous
doers and tellers and scribes of any
action of ours, whispering
      scintillation of the actual air —

we set out from here, this is our point of departure.
This "here" is our horizon, our
encapsulated vista of realizable landscape,
first step toward ecstatic transfiguration into
peacock-tailed magnificent nothingness, our first
step at a
    crossroads of spectacular energy,
our heart scooped out like a large papaya and replaced with
      divine filling,

our uncritical, careless trilling rapture like the
dawn birds now on their momentary branches outside my door,
no inhibitions in those
  bird-yelps, leaps, loops, bips, bleeps,
blasts of song, long and short
    take-offs and
      landings, each hover
   and landing a new departure point, each
point of departure a
    new flight.

                                                 4/20-24

WHITMAN'S DEATHBED

for Lamont Steptoe

I lay down on Walt Whitman's deathbed in the upstairs bedroom
of his house in Camden, New Jersey, when the
    enthusiastic Parks Department curator and my
        wife went out of the room and down the
            narrow, well-worn
    rickety stairs with its hand-smoothed bannister,

I took the opportunity in all coolness and calm
to lie down on the fresh white bedspread (certainly modern)
and settle down on the mattress (also no doubt new),
but the wooden bed original with simple
        rounded bedposts Whitman's carpenter father
      made for him, in the room he
        died in, under the
same white ceiling looking out of the
    same window he did, in this very spot going over the
        Deathbed Edition of *The Leaves of Grass* —

I sank into a gray fuzziness in the room of it, his
narrow house in Camden swept clean and
    tidy for visitors, not like he
      liked it, a literary
rat's nest of books and papers and
important documents, Emerson's original congratulatory letter
    helter-skelter in a pile somewhere, photos of
Tennyson tacked to the wall, a little stucco
    statue of Grover Cleveland downstairs by the

      fireplace, pictures
with more pictures tucked into their frames
    (Whitman's frames never big enough!) —

no one in the house but me, the guide
    and my wife now, they
chattering downstairs, Walt's bedroom quiet, endless,
ceiling the same, floorboards the same
    (his dusty slippers in a
      glass case downstairs in the dining room),
window out on the
world the same — how many
  people have passed by this bed, or wanted to,
    when Walt was alive or dead,
      even as now, as I
lie here, the room's accoutrements different, the
street outside widened and
    noisy with cars, bridges, pavements,
kids, gulls, skies, Pattersons, Nerudas, Ginsbergs, redwoods,
prairies, healthy, muscular men in
     overalls, wholesome, loving women in
    aprons, ponds, rivers, paddle boats, gunfire,

the long Civil War corridors of beds on either side where
     sweet soldiers waited for Walt to kiss them to
       die, wounds, pails of black
blood, smells of sweat and wet wool, Walt in his
    chair by this very
      window, coverlet up to his
chin, under that
waterfall beard Lorca saw butterflies in,

Walt's eyes like two lit tunnels buses full of
    Iowa tourists or Kansas Bingo Clubs barrel through on their
way to Atlantic city unmindful of their glory, his mouth the
Barbaric Yawp hooked up now to
    TV networks arching over the whole world
      24 hours a day,
his big body now become partly
  paralyzed and emaciated as those
    soldiers' were,
as shaky as America is, whose enterprise has always been
dubious in this world, but whose
  people have a deep capacity for
      wisdom nonetheless —

old wispy-haired Walt on his deathbed with
    palsied hand,
  erasing, writing over lines in pencil,
adding a few lines more for one last
    stab at it, veined hand shaking, a
    few final statements, under this
very ceiling, in this very bed with its
four solid legs footed firmly on the
    second floor bedroom in Camden, New Jersey, slate gray
      day on Mickle Street — I could

lie here forever, dear Walt,
    but I get up.

I get up. But I could
lie here forever.

                                        4/28

SOME POEMS I WOULD LIKE TO WRITE

for Jim Cory

1 The Pen

A giant fountain pen leans against a mountain,
  golden tip pointed upward, point dipped
    into pellucid blue of sky-ink,
and the shank, as all shanks must, gravity-
    bound, lies against the
      angle of the mountain as if strapped to it.

A cluster of classical architecture spreads out
around the base where the
  pen shank touches level ground: Greek, so
marbled and mathematical; Hindu, so
  vegetable and cosmic (giant rock broccoli
    standing straight up with carved
      naked deities holding on for
    dear life around their stems);
then assorted yak-skin yurts, ice-block igloos, magnificent
  mosques of blue tiles blending into
    blue sky to the point of
      sheer invisibility;
plus some earth-mounds, sloppy ones like moles live in,
or mysterious sinewy shapes of snakes along flat ground
  like the ones in Ohio, or strange stick-figure men with
    giant sketched erections
etched in the dirt in Dorset, not
    visible except from

    high up in the air — some levitation
        that graphic artist must have had
  to supervise a figure of such perfection, indecipherable
        at eye-level.

All of earth's semiotic literature
  spread out around the
    base of that pen tilted on the mountain's slope
while melting rivulets crash around it,
  as if the whole living orb of creation were
    tuning up to let the
      pen be its mouthpiece.

But the blue, the pellucid blue of the sky, is its
    slate, the blood of
      clouds and
    space its ink, cotton of
clouds, carbon of stormy weather, lightning
    intuitions its reason for being.

Now the pen's in gear — a shiver runs through it —
  ready to write.

2 The End

Strike the gong. *Ready to*
  write! Enough procrastination to build
ten well-engineered suspension bridges in,
enough putting-off of the grand sweep
  to die and be buried in for

ten thousand years, then get up from that
   morbid horizontal, shake off the
      topsoil, and look around uncomprehending
at people walking on points, propellers on their
   heads, little
      rockets keeping them aloft, and
sirens everywhere, against an artificial blue sunlight.

I'm so tired, and my bones ache,
I haven't read enough to know enough about
   anything, done enough, sat enough in front of
those who know to ask the right
      questions, but this life we're encased in

goes on, rolling us
   thoughtfully to the
      end.

3 The List

O.K. Now I'm
   ready to roll with this
poem about all the poems I'd like to write, like
one about stairways, some going up, some going down, and
   all the great historical personages on them
      either ascending or descending, emblems of their
         time —

or one that begins as an adventure, very contemporary,
a setting off across town or across

country. Then another completely
       different poem blooms out of the
            middle of that one, about alchemy in
    China, or transcontinental
       ballooning, one character remaining the
same, then another poem blooms from the entrails of
that one, violent and destructive as a
            Japanese hurricane, passions and
bloodthirstiness taking over completely, very Gothic,
and then *blam!* Out of the guts of that one
    another, slow and beautiful, sinuous as
       sunlight, like the stalk of a
    toadstool on a high valley ridge, almost
            transparent, almost
            not there at all except for its
wild smell of sweet semen,
and out of that still point a return to
the original narrative, same guy doing the same
thing, crossing
   town or country in search of his
      wingéd shoes, or his
         train ticket to Le Néant — Nothingness —
poof into oblivion on a melodic high note!

Someone did a long poem about the elephant —
I'd like to do a long poem about the bee,
getting right into a bee's life, mob scenes in the
            hive, solemn approach
    down those hexagonal corridors to the throne room,
audience with her Majesty the Bulbous Egg-layer,
grunting with swollen eyes nearly closed, the

squirt-sound of eggs coming out her behind as we
talk in slow whispers about the weather, how the
lay of the land looks, prospects for a good
    pollen harvest, the climate for
      world peace, that
        sort of thing.

Or a poem that explores the human body inch by inch, from
inside and outside, dives like those
    miniature scientists in that early 60's movie
      through the bodily bloodstream — the
    heart, apotheosis of human
history and existence's all-seeing
    consciousness being in the
absolute center of it, seeing down all its
cathartic vascular corridors into splendors beyond this
life's time and space, God's elegant porches, His
    celestial proclamations to make
that particular rainbow moth-wing, that clustering
    chrysanthemum, those
particular African children dancing inside a circle of
      glaring red shrubs,
each speck of dust raised as we walk, floating again
down, then
situate the poem back outside the
body, re-inhabited with the Spirit of Pure Light,
  able to do the Any-World Fandango Blues
    Charisma Shuffle, kissing the
lips of cosmos with a baby's true tenderness!

I actually want to start that poem right now —

but, no — maybe not yet. It's late and I feel
my spirit flagging. I'd need
gallons of honey from that bee poem I could
  suck up my proboscis to get the
    strength for those visions!

These are epic poems I envision, and it's
extra hard work because I have to
envision people patient enough to listen to them!
That's the big task! Where have all the
   people gone? Bubbles of worlds appear on
all our lips, but instead of
transferring them to someone else's, they float
up into the air and finally
    slip into the
      air, completely invisible,
         — *gone!*

Help me, other poets, youths or stronger elders!
I feel like I'm slipping deep down into steam.

Eels and garter-snakes writhe completely around me.
Have you got tons of self-confidence? Enough to
turn a phrase just so, hold it
  up to cool light, let light
    filter down through its
      pure
        clarified amber?

WHEN I GET TRANSFORMED INTO A WOMAN

> *'Tis. 'Tis. Ytis!*
> *Actaeon...*
> *   and a valley*
> — Ezra Pound (Canto IV)

When I get transformed into a woman
my lips will be real roses, my ears small white
   cowrie shells curved and smooth as glass. My
  breasts will flare in the early morning
     African sun as I sway back to
   camp with a corrugated tin water bucket on my head.

When I get transformed into a woman
the fat that grows around my man's belly and
   waist in middle age
will accumulate around my buttocks and thighs,
soft as stuffed silk and smooth as combed sand.

When I get transformed into a woman
I will wear clothes no one dared wear —
streamers edged in sheet-metal,
hats of acetylene torches shooting blue flames —
go as topless as an Etruscan acrobat,
the cool eyes of a tigress and the steely eyes of a lady lion-tamer both
    rolled into one. I see myself in
  tight black leather, long black hair ablaze, entering the
      cage in the center ring — slow, muted drum roll —
    skittish beasts on boxes, the crowd hushed,
my entire feminine-once-masculine psyche ground to a stupefied

THE PUZZLE · 45

      halt before the
    prospect of being torn apart by the
teeth of angry lions, in public! *Ah,*
        delicious dismemberment!

When I get transformed into a woman
will I be treated like a lady? (I'll
    shave my beard)
When I get transformed into a woman
will I get shown to the best table
   next to a window overlooking the
      piazza? Will my
anonymity as a man be suddenly transformed as
well into high-profile recognition for the
    sheer courage I've exhibited by just
      being alive! (What will my
wife and children think? My dear addled
   mother, will she remember? My
brother, the lawyer, will he somehow
     get me cut out of the will? My
school records, will they get mysteriously
      lost, my
   job résumé, shredded every time I
      go to apply?)

When I get transformed into a woman
I will want that fake white ermine everywhere,
on car-seats, sofas, even suits and slacks of
    white ermine — no
      peasant taste for me!

When I get transformed into a woman
will my present tense obstacles to clear thinking
   be gone, will I have an
easier time concentrating with a female mind than I
      do now?
Will it open up new possibilities for
   intellectual adventure and spiritual
      search, or will doors
   slam all down the hall, one
after another, smartly clicking locked?

Will getting transformed into a woman
   this late in life (I'm 52 this year)
      bring me back my lost youth?
Will it be like sky-diving, jumping from an
      open exit into the blue, no chute
fluttering out until the last
   minute, or not at all (these are the
      risks we have to take)?

Will all my poetical works become obsolete to this moment,
my man-visions cancelled by my being
   reborn out of the womb of my own body into its
opposite, head the same, but the
      world heading this way
         spectacularly different? Will I
view things differently, from unbefore-seen
      angles and emotional
         undulations, the loud complaint of
women at the end of this
century now become also my own? My

own head held high in this fray, lending my
hormone-harmonized voice, now without its
low testosterone guttural, to the general choir?
Will I suddenly understand the oppression,
and see, having tasted both sexes, a possible
      opening?

Will some things become easier? Will
   crying be less a rare ecstatic release for me,
and more a feminine lubricant for the
    unyielding materiality of this world,
the futility and frustrations of our daily tasks?

Will
prayer be easier, now become totally woman before
God's pulsing Light? Bride in reality at last to His
audible wave-band! Letting Light enter and take up
   engendering residence in me, unknown by
     others, unseen except by Him?

Glints out on the lawn under the
   rain tonight are warm and
      dark in their star-like flickerings.
I let out my long black hair, go out onto the
newly wet grass, kneel with soft knees
on earth's lustrous strands, its all-encompassing
    coiffure of nature, sweeping away as far as
the eye can see, grass blades bowing in homage to the
still sea in
    sensuous moonlit delicacy.

I left the children tucked in their beds.
I crept out on bare feet.
My pink silk slip clings to my thighs.
I incline my body and am lifted and
   carried over
waves blowing like tent-tops. Voices

croon as I pass. Soft female voices, melodious
   as grass.

I rise from the dark and find
my legs trees, my hands
radiant leaves, my own voice
braiding streams, my eyes lights above
   cool water,

my transformed body
   resplendent

     among clouds.

                               5/30-6/1

BE IN A FOREIGN COUNTRY

One way to alleviate a difficult situation
is to imagine you're living in a foreign country,
that the racket outside is people speaking a
    strange language, that
  the food you are eating is actually a rare dish whose
history goes back to
early royalty or the myth of the first potato,
sumptuous table set under a tree for the arrival of the last
outrigger of the fleet.

The light angling into the front room window
is from sunlight slanted over
    another continent, that
      down on the street
donkeys laden with firewood pass, or llamas
   laden with wool, an elephant with its
      mahout swinging a liberal stick and
shouting hectic guttural shouts, not the
        passing of a diesel truck!

A river flows at the end of the street where the
women gather before dusk to tell their latest gossip,
   the horns you hear across
town are not another traffic jam, but
   a wedding celebration that
     goes on for a week where the
       merrymakers go from house to house,
or a funeral celebrated not with mourning but with dances of joy.

That at the end of the day
your night falls on another country entirely, maybe
  Tahiti if it's
warm enough,
    Iceland if it's not.

In the morning
you will peel a surprising fruit whose
    taste you've never experienced and whose
      name you do not know.

In the afternoon you will visit
never-before seen countryside. Peasants
  walking back with their sheep
    will greet you by name with shining teeth.

Bats will swoop at dusk into the night sky.

An all-white owl will turn its
face to you
  and blink

    one eye.

6/11

THE MAN FROM PORLOCK

For I have also been visited by the
   man from Porlock,
he knocked on the door as I
   slid out the birth canal, he
diverted me from contemplation of
   Paradise by an
      endless monologue about Life Insurance.
The fact that his
paranoid words choked me
   nearly to death didn't
      dawn on him.
He usurped my sphere of childhood's grassy knolls
   by false history lessons and
      patronizing social studies projects —
the curtains of Paradise closing over innocence's visions of an
unearthly brilliance with
   photo-realism and the
      forcing onto me of a world view only
severely brain-damaged folk confined to small
      windowless cells could have.

The man from Porlock in the same gray
   tweeds he wore when he
interrupted Coleridge from *Kubla Khan*
to a doorway in half-light with a 4-dimensional
   rather than multi-dimensional man standing in it,
into whose dull eyes vast vistas of silver-edged
glory were sucked faster than the
   downfall of Rome and the

  soupy burial of Pompeii, whole
   lavender and gold and turquoise
    skylines absorbed, the ones I also
saw from the ripening canyons of my heart as a youth,
backdrops of orient towers and displays of
  love's fireworks over a silhouette of
   minarets and prickled rooftops,
with that sound,
that rush of cascades like dulcimer notes,
that leonine roar reaching back to a
mouth as wide as the origin of the entire creation, ecstatic
leap through the stars outlining every creature created, our own
links to songbirds obvious, bulbuls in
  onyx trees singing their hearts out,
bower birds painting thatched entranceways blue
   with feathers in their beaks.

The man from Porlock knocked at the
beginning of our life stunting imagination, and
stands at the end ready to sell us an
  expensive burial — for some
   reason, his totally unmagnetic personality
    only the most
God-intoxicated can resist,
his gray face, blank eyes, thin lips, lank
hair, droning voice — why do we know
  more about him after all
than about the pleasure dome and dulcimer
   decreed to be our everlasting
    legacy?

What has let us let him draw us to his cold knock out of the warm riches of original visions of perfection?

Why do we ascribe to him so much
    reality?

Why is this life a lesson in
    loss of liberty?

                                                          6/17

SLEEP AND WAKING

What do we do in order to sleep?
  Sheer tops off mountains, hammer
sky into pewter, indulge in
sexual fantasies personified in
giant gelatin shapes filled with warm oil, suck milk from the
    dry wool of sheep, descend into
  cellars of blue velvet, slip star-shaped
crystals under our eyelids and exchange the
rolling green valleys of our bloodstreams for some
    cheap pictures and a single
swaybacked horse swatting flies. All this to
bed down for the night. As well as bomb a few
   towns, terrorize a few
     villages, write
midnight treatises on warfare. Forget to
plant lilies on mass graves. Go deeply into

sleep, a sleep a thousand, thousand disembodied
souls pass through on their way to a
black river. A black windmill against a
black sky. Their faces gaunt and
unsmiling. No sound. That's

the sleep of this millennium. Shards of
angular metal sticking up out of
soft angelic waves. Glints of
cold steel sparkles off the surface of
dark coffee in a white cup.

All this to get cozy for a long winter's nap.
Pull the town's gospel choir over our
heads in the form of rough quilting, pull the
idealisms of the young high school teacher
over our faces in the form of a
thick black pillow, just to get some
   shut-eye. We sink into the

material world to sleep as if we were part-
owners of it, as if anything we held onto tight enough
would last, as if the
   minutes of our lives could be pulled out forever like
     taffy. A sun
 rises on our sleep and finds us
deeply sleeping.

But what do we do to wake up?

There's a cone of bright snow that fits snugly over our heads
in the center of a red cyclone.
There's an emblematic lion with erect head
whose eyes are long golden beams.
There's a water for splashing the face that
evaporates into touches of exceptional
   mercy. There's a long
     ladder. Rungs of transparent
silver. Propped up against a rotting shack and a
broken-down fence. There's a singing hook to the
heartbeat that gets it to leap over a
   lump as large as the Himalayas.

These are some of the things we do to wake up. A lightbulb
naked as ice, soothing as rain, a
book opened to the page where
matter melts through every stick of furniture
   into a little wood the
Eternal Procession has just passed through, Dame
     Gratitude at the lead, a deer with trembling
hooves at each side of her, Hope and Fear, a sprig of amber
   held up between her
     forefinger and thumb. A
radiance. An eye like an
open window facing a canyon of floating white clouds. A

skeleton in the closet of our flesh
turning to shivers of sheer ivory. A

silence of outer space that slips in between our
silences.

A light playing on the surfaces of our faces
like low mist over dark marshes.

6/20

MIDDLE OF THE NIGHT

I get up in the
   middle of the night and follow the
     long cave down the stairs,
        past the sleeping
bears, Madame Trieste and her
   band of Gypsies camped in the
      living room (they're on their
way back to Rumania via the
uncertain fortunes of American cities — their
trained bear is asleep in his leather muzzle by the
pillowed sofa), and as I
go through this
sudden 3 a.m. summer swelter down from the
bedroom where I could feel insomnia's
     masseurs of a constant
  low-grade annoyance kneading my flesh enough to keep me from
sinking back to sleep next to my
    sleeping wife, sinking down through that
illumined gray angle of dull sweetness into soft sleep,

I step down stair by stair
past Teutonic mythology waiting in the wings for another
grand historic appearance, Harold of
    Macedonia with his
       ill-equipped troops (they're all asleep!)
enduring the night before a sunrise bivouac into
   non-existent space and total disappearance.

The elements are curled up in the dark as I descend,

fire bites its knuckles and dreams of forests, but a
    quiet house will do,
water slinks around through domestic pipes and drains
     happy to be near,
air flattens itself out in four dimensions, sinking
   in and out of peoples' lungs and the
      lungs of every living creature down to the
        tiniest mite,

and the earth
that opens up to swallow me as I lightly step down
stairs through the otherwise sleeping
house to my cool basement couch by the
open screen door where
I-don't-know which gargoyles or angels
   stand me guard against any
     further encroachments of the
       night, earth

lightly
closes over me as I finally
settle down to sleep.

                                              7/9

RIMBAUD IN ADEN

1

The pink roofs and the sun on the mud,
the knife on the edge of the table,
the doorway, the food, the few sticks and tough bread,
heat like an oven. The
heat like an oven. Nothing quite
like it. The heat. Everything

outlined by heat. Transforming the
world. Rimbaud closes his eyes to slits and
thinks. He's got big hands. He's
black as a native now. Become his

book.

2

Off into anywhere. He
wanted to escape the West. Well,
he did. Nothing
quite like it. Some sand and rocks and
the heat. He's
totally different. Straight-backed.
Determined. To the end of night.
Independent. Full of plans.

We don't envy his

apprenticeship with
this extent of privation. A
desert saint, blessed with
fever. Always penniless. A
monk might have been
easier. He's cut away
everyone. Every comfort and
support. Makes mad
journeys. Among well-known
killers of white men. No one
kills him but Reality. Slowly.

Gritting his teeth as
tight as the edge of a scimitar.

No one follows him there.

READING ONESELF

Like going down a mine shaft in Siberia —
  machinery's old, tunnels low and airless,
conditions generally horrible, coal-dust everywhere
   tar-papering your lungs into
    early mummification, light a mere
  glimmer, but part of a
family tradition goes back to grizzled grandfathers and
  convict great-grandfathers, down into the
    dark shafts.

Taking out a piece of my own writing to see what.
  the test of time has
   done to it, instead of reading a poem by,
    say, Yannos Ritsos, trying to
     suit it to my
      mood, but
taking the autobiographical descent, going down into a
   familiar hole, into the
dark earth as down
  into one's own body, seeing the
crazy pictures a too-long maintained squatting
   position brings about, steamed up
    landscapes, steam-heated
     interiors, steamy shadows against
      gauzy curtains, a real *"Memories of Things Past"*
police lineup of familiar faces and mistaken identities —

we read ourselves to find out
  where we've been, take the

      pulse of the dying
patient, and it shows that behind our
   usual silhouette-heads and their
      usual slanted latitudes might well unroll a
paisley vista of new plateaus, or thoughts hollowing themselves
out at a touch to be cool
   incandescent silver and
      easy to see through.

Take your two arms and wrap them around your chest,
take a deep breath, take your feet and press them
   cross-legged into the ground, take your
eyes off the road for a second and experience
   avalanche car-crash immensity into
God's grand speedway past mile high columns of
   pure cloud.

Welcome to the pre-embryonic Classical mode.

Welcome to your natural altitude.

                                                    7/29

BODY-LOCK

We're stuck in our bodies.
We can't just walk away from them
    except by dying.
We're locked in a maximum security genetic prison.
We can't really change the way we look, Michael Jackson and
    Phyllis Diller notwithstanding, we
       can't totally transform our
basic stature, our basic girth.
And, you may ask, why would anyone want to?
But I have this physical longing to be

  tree, cloud, eagle,
      tissue-thin butterfly wings in an updraft.

Still body of clear water.

The material zombie-lock, the bone-cabinet and
    flesh-dress, the face-lock, gesture-lock,
color-lock, until death. Even facial-
    expression-lock, like our father-mother, slope-
       shouldered or straight-
          backed like the
great-great-grandfather in the faded tintype.
We go all the way back. Flesh-lock, blood-lock, bone-
    structure-lock. The physical configuration
       hurling its atomic
Morse code lariat to our tongues and eyelashes
all the way through all the interlinked loins and wombs from
Adam and Eve onward.

But this is not us. We strain and become
   tired. We push against the
walls we find ourselves in. But
we are really
tree, cloud, eagle,
bright butterfly wings in an updraft,

even body of clear water. The tissue between us
   falls apart, becomes transparent, lets us
through from the gene-pool to God's
original Glance onto the
   momentary space of creation. His
gaze that fell onto the genetic progression
for the purpose of knowing Him, person by
   upright person, laugh by
     cry, name by nameless one

up to us at this exact moment on our
     own edge of bodily existence.

It's a green place, with rolling hills.
Goes all the way up to the
  sky.

Body-lock.

Sky-lock.

7/31

STRIPES

for Michael & Judy Lorimer

1

On the shoulder of the creature of the blackest evening
after the collision of astral furniture with the
plumbing fixtures of descent,

a globe of intensest silver floats on
    a face of indigenous delight.

What has this got to do with New York? There are
tickets given away for ringside seats to the
    Apocalypse of Rational Thought,
there are golden ropes that demarcate
    the exact spot of the Birth of Time —
sidewalks go everywhere at once in all directions at once
    like frightened spiders,
and animals lost to the fossil record
appear bashfully for a moment in the smoke-like
    outlines of shadows
cast on the pavements
    by a million hurrying New Yorkers.

Leaves as large as landscapes and as green as the ocean deeps
fall across this urban vision

and pedestrians in ripped clothes inhale the
    freshness of chlorophyllian antipodes.

2

Shea Stadium Faux Haiku

Sparrows at the Mets game
   perch on some net-mesh strung to a pole,
     scan the crowd below
through what eyes?

Players in uniform
   play their hearts out.
People around them
     clap and shout.

Sun slants on the stadium.
   Plane overhead.
Sparrows on the net-mesh
   — gone.

3

On the train back to Philadelphia
   past little fertile backyards and
     broke-window'd factories and a
green and yellow swamp by a rust-girder'd bridge,

I am overwhelmed by a desire to write a poem so filled with
a kind of folkloric surrealism, Serbian-Turkik,
   Afghani-Nilotic, encapsulating those
last few hours in the Natural History Museum —

I want bright red horses leaping through neon clouds,
   clown sages costumed in layers of brass bells,
fountain-fires you put pots of sand in and
   draw out bunches of white roses,
windows you open out into the night and
stars with round faces come singing in.

No sound of voice too slight nor facial gesture too subtle
is lost, no
   word spoken directly from the
     heart lost in the
     on-flow of rushing air past the
forward motion of our lives — a tree of
     assembled bones, a shout of
live marrow
   establishing itself in time.
A sentence nailed in the air by a bearded
   carpenter with leather apron, eyeglasses of
triangular pearl lenses, like abalone so
   highly rubbed it
     finally becomes transparent.

These words cause
   some people to dance, some to
     die. Some
    come alive, a loaf of blue bread
     held on their lips with the
      tiny human glue of
the endless desire to survive.

Some of the red horses turn into roomy neon

   stalls at the end of the land.

Some stand still under a
     fall of black water.

Some speak in musical syllables
     only clouds understand.

4

It comes back in the mind! this
   New York of the senses, these
      angular stratagems! Towers and
elevators of cloud! Foxes in two-piece suits
   and sinister grandmothers, Innocence in black
      insouciantly walking along.
Jagged skyline contour against multi-colored sky
   videoramas, as

down below the reverse heaven of daily life each day
goes by in its delirious disguises.

Here's the spirit of a wounded elephant
   in a dreadlocked man with folded magazine.

Here's an arching song of white angels
   in a group of hand-holding schoolchildren entering
     the Natural History Museum.

Here's a man and woman standing together at a light

with miles of sand-blown Sahara between them
    through which phantom warriors replay
      the bloody chaos of their last massacre.
Taxis go by, nuns go by, lizards go by, small
    flying insects go by, giant diesel trucks go by,

nothing gets by
the material net
without glancing directly into the eyes of the
    divine game-plan at least
      one point in its life,

and this is what we saw between the hedges,
this is the lurid and placid foliage that
   blossoms and spreads in
     plain air there

come back into the mind
and gone out of the mind again

into a spot in Central Park, one
   tiny patch of ground, never
touched by a living presence,
never trod upon by even ant or rustled by
   breeze or hammered by
rain or lit by

lightning.

                                 8/3-5

ROCK

A rock has only one side.
Moonlight slathers white frosting
onto that side
   night after night.
Deer walk slowly past it with
thin hoofs ticking through
   old snow.

A face hovers near the surface of that rock —
a fine face of resplendent light.

A house has many doors and windows.
Stairways inside transport people up and down
   to their destinations.
A house sits securely on its foundation
   on earth
  above a molten core.
People sit around tables inside the house on earth
chewing and arguing
  in bodies secure
   around molten cores.

A heart sits and beats like a living rock
in the middle of a lake of light.

With each beat a creature opens newborn wings
   and takes off in flight.

Winding roadways lead up to it

and straight down away from it.

There are always lengthy processions of people
   winding around the rocky mountainside
     waiting to have an audience
        with the heart,

as if a light sliced through it to reveal the
resplendence of its
serene molten core, its
core of clenched diamond, its
core of open space.

A hand reaches out
to take another hand.

A face bends down to gaze
into another face.

                                                      8/19

ATLANTIC CITY NATURE POEM

1

On the Atlantic City Boardwalk
I want to write a poem about
    remote pristine nature.

Sitting at an outdoor table watching
    a million people pass by,
some shaking hands with a Mr. Peanut in sneakers with
    top-hatted friendly-faced
        molded plastic figure over his body,
(boy's face inside
    visible through the monocle),
various people walking a
    single Pekinese, various people passing each other
in lithely whooshing wheelchairs, well-dressed Oriental woman in
    Dragon Lady black dress and stiletto black
        heels in broad daylight! Guffawing, back-slapping
blond jocks in sporty shorts, people walking along reading a
    guidebook speaking Korean, a
    huge black man in bright fuchsia shorts and bright mustard
        undershirt pushing his
    tiny round baby in a tiny white pushchair,

and I want to write about mountainpeaks rising
blue above clouds, mist
wisping around them in gauzy puffs,
geysers gushing from the center of the sea, or the
delicate mating habits of hummingbirds!

The Atlantic waves crash, the Atlantic gulls
    cackle and jibe,
rubber sedan-chair wheels ripple and rumble on the
    wooden slats of the boardwalk

and I want to see a pointed peak of pure crystal through clouds so
high of actual altitude that the natural color spectrum pales,
watch the stealth of the
white Siberian tiger against stretching miles of white snow,
and see the slow fall of the aurora borealis beyond this
slowly turning planet's darkening edge.

2

Driving back from Atlantic City along the expressway at night
after our hours' long trek from one end to the
   other of the boardwalk, past the columned cement
     rotunda overlooking the sea where the
Miss America Pageant is held, past the
   bust of John F. Kennedy facing the boardwalk itself and the
     tackiest aspects of America,
walking along the shore's edge, eleven year old daughter
   barefoot in the great Atlantic's froth
     picking up perfect shells,
walking out to the twinkling Ferris wheel on Steel Pier where
carny types yell at us to win a prize, those
universal misfits with microphones and cigarettes
   who've maybe spent their
     miserable lives running away from miserable love,
my wife and daughter and I

walked until our legs felt like brittle lath stilts
making our first visit to the
    wild Atlantic shore.

Standing there
watching our daughter bend down to pick up a shell
my wife and I simultaneously think
— we've lived on both sides of the Atlantic —
    England and now Philadelphia,
and both sides of the American continent, for eight years in
    Santa Barbara right
      next to the green Pacific,

and now we stand here in our
   brief selves

like polar bears cavorting in snow,
like moths lost in a clothes closet,
like nails driven into a house that
   won't last forever,
like disembodied voices adrift above the chill Atlantic sea
    as distant stars come out

and policemen start patrolling under the boardwalk with
flashlights
  to chase away stray lovers and any sleazy stragglers

and the Ferris wheel winks dark
and the Gypsy crystal balls are covered over with cloths
    embroidered with roses,

it all behind me now as I struggle to keep awake on the expressway back home to the

slowly opening green softness
  down the road

(with slanted light-beams coming out of it)

of my own terrestrial grave.

8/22-23

ANNUNCIATORY ANGEL

From the office picnic-table at lunch, over the
   top of a neighboring bush, I've been observing
  a flowering tree whose bunches of
     white flowers I first noticed
as brilliant snowy feather-dusters at the tips of
      branches splaying out like spikes,
the whole tree vaguely tropical — here in
      Pennsylvania — something
Gauguin might have painted behind a Tahitian maiden
    as a striking decorative motif —

but today those bunches of white blooms have
   evidently gotten so heavy
     their branches are weighed down and forlorn-looking, the
       flowers brown and
gloomy as old war refugees, barely
   visible now behind the flat-topped bush they used to
splay so proudly over, the wind
     occasionally blowing their hunched
       arches up into view.

The day is overcast. Falling leaves make descending diagonal
   lines through the air
     blown off their trees, ever-so-slowly
twisting diagonally down finally
      to the ground.

There's a slate hugeness of sky —
and one would half-expect the

    blinding brightness of all that
vast gray to open up onto the
       extended figure of an
    annunciatory angel with accordion dark blue wings and
face like a billowing furnace, arms open wide,
   translucent patterns of color like a
      rainbow robe circulating around its
    silken body as wide as the entire sky, saying,
"All's finished now," the

flowering tree bent forward to
hear, the wind a
high whistling, listening,
the stones and grass silent, the air
      suddenly still.

                                             9/3

SMALL ENIGMATIC POEM

The rain came
  in the shape of a barn,

the road came
  in the shape of a car,

the bride came
  in the shape of a
    sexual coin,

so what shape are we in?

The window came
  in the shape of a tree,

the house came
  in the shape of an old man
    and woman,

the river came
  in the shape of a flood
    of circular saws,

so what shape are we in?

AIRLINE FLIGHT 774

There are things we might do differently
   miles high in the air above the clouds with their
     blinding whiteness puffing just below us
on airline Flight 774 to Kansas City, Missouri

because at any moment we might die —

On the one hand, given the choice between
   omelette and pancakes, we might choose
pancakes, hang the sugar,
     forget the cholesterol!

because at any moment we might die —

slather on the syrup, gobble the apple-filled croissant,
drink the metallic coffee, because if
time is short what does it matter if we
bloat up like one of those clouds down below, our
   heart has been sweetened, our mind
appeased and our
palette tickled by the airline's executioner's breakfast
(which sudden end, of course, could just as easily happen
   any time below, sitting at our
breakfast table at home in our
     cozy bungalow).

But, on the other hand, because at
   any moment we might die
(There's nothing like the prospect of being executed to

    concentrate the mind),
the heart may focus in and in to a cupped domain of shaded
      light and
freshest air, a
   temple with crystal steps appear outlined in
    shimmering prismatic hues, golden twitching
      electrical fringes of
   feathery incandescence surrounded by
   singing birds, and inside the
beating dome of almost invisible columns and
     celestial panels
  the Divine Name repeat itself
     by Itself

  to sustain our breath and
    allay our grief that at
      any moment we might die —

that at any moment our plane might lose altitude, might
     nose-dive
  down and down in a spiralling
    watery coil through miles and
miles of white cloud to a definitive
     perfect
       landing right at

     God's Feet.

9/5
(over Pittsburgh)

AVALANCHE

"An avalanche that falls up?" exclaimed the
 bewildered magistrate. "Rocks the size of
Mt. Aetna, falling skyward? What's the
 point?" "Such lightness of heart's
 the point," saith Gravity.

Oh, I rowed out across the Lake of Patience
with my two usual oars of Frustration and Despair
and the Lake of Patience accommodated me, held me
 up, finally even
sucked me into its greater being. The boat
 broke, the oars got lost, I
 drifted along on that lake and longed to be
 dragged out to sea — the
Sea of Patience — bobbed out on its languid
 ebbs and flows.

"Not so fast!" shouted the trees at the end of our
 street, in unison. A formidable chorus, trees,
 no slouches at close harmony.
"Root here, root here! Let that wanderlust shoot
 down into black soil. Branches will
 finger out, bark
 grow to shield them, flying
birds use you for rest and nesting."

(Trees almost always speak in
rough classical meter, being trees.)

Lightness of heart's the point. Lightness as in a
closed dark room whose door has been

    suddenly flung open.

9/9

DEATH

Death, if you had to enter a popularity contest
   I'm sure you'd win last place. And
     yet, you're more an
intimate part of us than our own names, which get
delicately taken from us at our
   deaths — like the tendril-thin skeletons of fried
     trout on a white plate by candlelight
        are lifted out with sensitive efficiency —
and their spindly letters entered
in registers and chiseled on headstones.

You are slid down inside us at birth, you
coolness, you unmentionable, and when I
   lose my way a little, if I
     address you seriously it seems to
ignite my wires and put me
   back on track. I

thought of you at prayer, that
   realignment of prow with current, as a
thrilling intimate to our
     flesh and bones, our blood's
       waterwheel which one day
   suddenly stops, you
absolute keeper of our singlemost important appointment,
      coming at us
with all the technicolor of the
    movie of our life, over a
      long bridge full of

      spectral traffic over
sluggish black water that might be
quiescent marble. Finger-prick! Dewlap! Who

hosts the most unsentimental reception,
  all our attributes of superficial courtesy
stripped away to reveal what mortals have
   always had to
      deal with, their own
         shrinkage, their own
horizontality to this world, perpendicularity
      to the Next,

no one quite prepared, O you death, love-hated by
    all, puckering up those
glossy too-red lips
      wet with the glisten of nothingness,
hovering fantastically in front of
     too-wide wings

that extend forward past the margins of our mortal
      windy edge.

10/31

FURTHER APHORISMS

"Three gates and one pond do not a country make."

*"Robert, Bob, and Bobby do not sit down to the
    same dinner."*

*" 'Click-click-swish' go the bamboo on their way to work, which is
    remaining rooted to one spot, being bamboo."*

*"The cliff grows higher as the
    suicide nears its peak."*

The king's mad aunt sat in the dust and drew
    death's head after death's head,
        gazing distractedly at the ends of her
            fingers and
screeching.
The aphorisms that held up the
    kingdom
    did not hold her.
Her frail face barely beclouded her ever
    frailer mind.

She had
farmed the land as a girl out in the provinces,
    she had learned the
    ancient wisdom at her
father's feet, he a
    bureaucrat and a soldier,
and keeper, for a time, of the Golden Archives.

She had matured early at the
   natural death of her mother, and
married, it is said, the
  true source of her madness: an evil
    youth with
      monarchic ambitions who had
sailed to the capitol from one of the
  outlying islands. He was, by all
standards, barbarian. He left her
dazed on their wedding night,
     decapitated his rival in the dark and carried the
  loose head by its two eye-holes
like a bowling ball, rolling it across the
      polished parquet before her.
She herself acted as if blind after that, and
sat in the corner of the
  west chapel, brown sunlight
slatting in through the small teak openings and
    striping the altar and its
      chugs of thick incense with alternate dark
      and light.

She drew death's head after death's head in the dust,
    and repeated, in
  schoolgirl singsong, the 2,786
ancient aphorisms:

"Twenty chickens in a yard can't sing a note — put one on the chopping block, and it'll sing opera."

"To build a building you must have brick and mortar —

courtesy is essential for
spacious friendships."

"The worm can't show off the latest fashions —
it has no hips!"

"Words of wisdom find no place
in a fool's dictionary."

11/13

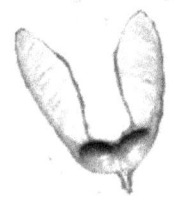

ON BEING A GUEST AT PUZZLE CASTLE

1

The rooms are cages for zoo animals.

You may open one of the
   heavy beveled doors and surprise a
     shy wildebeest at toilette,
a pair of giraffes rubbing together the longitudinal
   lengths of their affection for each
     other, flexible
 necks with those gazelle heads on them,
   eyes so big and moist
 you might see the curvature of the
    earth in the sheen of their
     reflection.

Walls covered with tapestries.
Corridor after corridor of cobbled stones,
   carvings in the molding of every ceiling of the
    entire history of the world from
pinpoint actual Big Bang burst onward to eventual
encounters in the dining room around sizzling
   sweetmeats, or chance meetings in the rose-smothered arbors
of back gardens, terrace upon green terrace down to the
    sea.

The ceilings themselves
show the whole universe upside-down, so that
gazing up into what you think is heaven

you find yourself looking into the
La Brea Tar Pits with its trapped fossils, or the
   lowest point at the bottom of the ocean,
those phosphorescent crawly things marking their
   slow unmistakable signatures across
      sluggishly swirling sand.

Well! No place for trivial pursuits at Puzzle Castle,
everything monumental! Every moment
  significant, as in
    great poems. Every episodic
  dot or grape or dust-mote or
    curl of smile or
      flick or fleck of
airborne message a symbol and representation of some
booming truth that aches until you
  grasp it full front with
    both hands, and maybe
  wraparound legs as well, but
      certainly the full
being, heart-beat throwing nets of its deepest
  comprehensions over the
    slightest significant twitch until

what opens out at last could only be described as
cavernous, space so resonant with the voice of
  silence even the
    tiniest branch of brittle
wintry bush
  extends its spiny entire length

out into it without
    fear of breaking.

2

Of course,
   none of this exits. It's a
pure construct out of
   the inordinate desire to
sit in a room with a lap desk on a
    rainy night in Philadelphia of all
      places and
let rise the rushing sides of phantasmagoric
   wonder that is this
actual castle of the puzzle, our
    dirigible craniums mostly
       filled with
     mental helium, and seen leaning in from an
edge never too far out of
   sight, the
  Generous Imager, pouring
    bounty from His
eternal pleasure into our

   pain.

3

Faces in half-shadow. Faces like

    half moons. One eye around a
      doorjamb. One eye in a
    goblet on the mantle. Spooky.

And me exhausted after my
return from a short lifetime of
  frustrated travel. I was

Rimbaud in Aden with those
  steely eyes of cold blue agate
clicking impatiently over a
    false bill of lading, another
      commercial prospect crushed.
I was there in the sandstorm giving my
  coat to a naked African. The fact that
in Paris gentlemen scholars in fur-lined
  overcoats were meeting in
    absinthe cafés to discuss my
      images never
  occurred to me, either
sleeping or waking. Asleep I was
    engulfed in dunes and forced to trek on
foot with weighty luggage, money tied to my
    sunken middle.
Awake I was forced to live the
  dream on the
    same feet through the
same unreal landscapes.

But I am not (thank God) him at all, and I
haven't arrived at Puzzle Castle in such a

    state of desperation. I've come here
eagerly, randily, hankering for the
   gold of imagery to loosen its
     liquid in my blood. No

dunes sail across this space, no
piles of rifles for Menelik II sit outside these
tent-flaps.

Only the sound behind me of the
  pilot light under the
    water-heater and, curiously,
a vivid sound of
  train-horn these
    ten or so blocks to the
      tracks.

The host of Puzzle Castle
is host of all worlds, whose
   perfect courtesy in
     all worlds demands a certain
obligatory courtesy from us in
   return.

Rain falls. The seasons revolve. Walls are
   scraped down to the
    barest minimum. Only rarely is a
  priceless fresco found under the
    first coat of paint. Only
rarely do we find we're living in a
   villa on the

      edge of Pompeii where the
rituals of the Mystery are
    carried out to perfection.

But this shouldn't stop us. Rainbows still
   catapult
     from our eyes.

11/25

SAINT SEBASTIAN AND SAINT JEROME'S LION

for Li-Young Lee

Saint Sebastian on his porch threw a
   bouquet of buzzards at the
     last bastion of evil thoughts that
   assailed him.
Saint Jerome's lion lay with chin on paws and
   agate eyes afloat
     near an open fire.
The night was filled to the brim with
   reverberations of distant splendor, the
     darkness closed around everything as if
   lined with ermine.

Goblets spontaneously fizzed. Bridges
   solid enough to walk on
     spontaneously appeared.
Between towers of yellow smoke and towers of blue ash
   bare Ethiopian dancers shook
     amulets to make
       gnats turn to fireflies,
         fireflies to fairies,
     fairies loop themselves into large
       white birds which flew in a
         slow flock toward the
       skylit tent-flap above us
and out along an incandescent edge
where sound
   emerges silken out of primordial grooves.

Saint Sebastian turned his
   transparent blue eyes back to see
      the Abyss open up in a fan and
         emit streamers of purple gas.

Saint Jerome's lion was dreaming of the
   spirit of his previous antelope coming through the
      tall grass to forgive him his
         violence and assuage any
           sorrow he might feel.

                                              12/2

TOES

Anyone who

knows

toes knows

poems.

                                        12/4

ON BEING A GUEST A PUZZLE CASTLE II

Now, this part of the poem has a
   bigger intention, an
     opening as of fields of waving stalks under
        coolness — daylight, birdsong, breeze.

It's as much inside Puzzle Castle as our
   earlier forays, but it is
trellises of flute music decorated with
   small blue flowers, it is
large waves pulsing apart as did those
  Red Sea waves for Moses, and we can
    stroll so casually on dry land
      between them
that one can see the vertical grain of water as if it were
transparent wood-panelling hurling itself
   skyward. Gulls
    wheel overhead. A bit of
     spray falls on us from
      tip-top fringes of suspended water,
   tassel droplets frozen in space, glinting in the
     noonday sun. We

walk down these avenues on mortality's urgent errands,
we exchange open glances, secret addresses,
   suspended heartbeats, and wear
sudden black hats and long black coats in slow procession past our
own features laid out flat along satiny mushrooms of
   crushed crystal, facial
     repose as fixed in a moment above the living as distant

                    stars,
the alive, remaining, shaped like
    paragraphs of chatter in a book
        surrounded by the
            spatial margins of death,
walk past with their
parenthetical clauses and imperfect
    punctuation, full stops and
        run-on sentences. We are
momentary nouns in a restlessness of verbs,

constantly throwing it all disgustedly
    behind us, pulling off the
        clumsy work gloves and
            cracked jackets of
labor and boredom to put soft soul-flesh on hot
    coals to walk across fire,

expressionless, unmoved by our
    own misfortunes. We need to be
unmoved by our own
misfortunes to see the
zebra streaks of pain across
another's features.

What began as wide-angle vision
ends with the expressive set of a mouth, the
exact seismographic look in an eye, an
exact thought hovering like
wide air around a
    heart.

12/8

DIVERSIONARY INTERLUDE FROM PUZZLE CASTLE

I just now realized I haven't the
    vaguest idea what a poem is.
For a while now I haven't
    felt like a poet.
 I've been feeling a bit like a
   porcelain bathing pan from which the dirty
     bath water's been
       thrown out.
Over the balcony. Into the
   street.

I'm sitting in a big swank bookstore slurping a
     cappuccino trying to
recapture what a poem's like. It
   should be a simple
    flexing exercise, heartbeat chin-ups, a
      couple of deep
thorax knee bends, extend my poor
uncertain self into molecular rainforest territories,
imagine the unimaginable, let my
   inner eyelids flutter in time to
     silver horse-hooves on glass,

take another sip,
look out over the browsers below the balcony railing,
finger the pages of the two poetry books I
   chose to drink coffee with,
hope for some success with this poem where more

worldly success eludes me, on purpose,
   casting the shadow of a
     short man on a
       tall wall,
wanting so much to burst full flower into
   Coleridgean expostulations, jubilant
     ignitions and re-ignitions, framed by the
reverse snowfall of silence, each image somehow
standing in the waterfall of its own radiance,
   as naked as a beautiful human body, but
clothed with the lights of meaning, a poem like a
combing of our thoughts into separate strands enough to
let the thought of the Greater Thinker slip
   in through the intervals, like
     silken water, like a
string of summer afternoons, like

sitting down after going around for nearly a
month feeling depleted and this
poem surging up from unknown depths,

everything that is
   remaining as it is
but with increased excitement, the

slow-motion constant astonishment of super-still
   contemplation, all
     matter in its shapes and textures falling
happily away into blossomings of
     immaterial flood.

I never harnessed myself to
    strict stanzas and meters,
crimping a message into a telegram
      shaped like a heart or an
         altar, preferring
naked light, fountaining images taking
their own shape in
    glittering descent.
It seems that plucking the ectoplasmic
    body out of the
air in its own
    form is what's
      asked of us now, yet I
admire the craftsman's cool aplomb, able to
    cast into clarified outlines any
thought or experience, at best
jewel-like, at the least its original
fiery tongue of nakedness
      tamed to the point of
         domesticity —
I see us all on a shore, hand in hand, licked by
    hot red surf,
intercommunicating by way of the
      oceanic clouds that
         cover us,

the drawing rooms and quiet conservatories are
down,

we're here at the mouths of volcanos,
wondering at our wrecks.

2

Is a poem a carefully calculated inspiration poured
   icy hot into the methodically arranged
      test-tube vials of someone
   else's pre-arranged form?
     Laboratory experiment in a
       hurricane?
Is a poem what goes on forever
  behind our eyes, but now

set out before them? Is it a

train of sky-atmospheres stopping to rest, down to the
bedraggled stations of earth-seasons?

Is it a trapped childhood busting out with
    adult fists? Is it a

conflagration suddenly bursting out in the middle of
   a flame, a chill growing cylindrical in the
     middle of an icicle, a

drop of stillness that stays
   suspended in the exact center of a desert of
total silence?

I think it might be thought of in
  some circles as the
    well-trained intellect
easily browsing among the classical themes and

betrayals of human endeavor,
but I never have enough time. The world is
showing a face of bereft traditions,
   aborigines in levis, lyre-bird feathers traded for
cheap imitations made in Taiwan, that the
  heart holds onto and lets go of the
    antelope leap of each alert moment
seeing the Face of God direct in the instant, the
first blinding flash of pewter in a thunder-roll of
common scrap metal,

it's a poem of edges, angles half-meshing, cogs, propulsions,
then sudden relief, when out of a
white field of beaten straw rises

one white pheasant, the last of its flock, as
white as the air, invisibly

flying.

TRAIN

If we could only get all the people we've ever
   known, even if only for a
     single intimate season, together, on a
train, say, going
   nowhere, all
present in the
    cars, not necessarily in
      chronological order, passing through

snow banks, or on the
   high Andes, although that's not
     really important, no, going
nowhere in particular, but all the

important people in our lives if we
   thought hard enough, the
bosomy Jewish girls with cozy kitchens in college where we
really discussed Wallace Stevens over one
coffee after another and
     lots of cigarettes —

all the people we exchanged
   ecstasies with, diving into the
   mystical reality of those
     corpuscular moments, rivers of
illumined amoebas and miraculous
      molecules, ribbons of
        elemental water, biological
signatures signed with utter

    solemnity on the
        flesh of another, reading another's
signature as well in the bargain, imprinted
    forever in our
        own flesh,

sphinx-like persons we never really knew,
extremely magnetic persons we
    now wish we'd known better,
persons with whom we communicated ultimate
    secrets, now wisped off into their own
        unknowns, although
existing, unless dead, somewhere on this
earth, a pocket of their
    consciousness still a part of
        the spectral coat we
ourselves wear until death —

what if we could walk down the
train-aisle between seats, and
everyone in those seats was
someone we once knew, once loved or
fantasized love over, once

spent blocks of time with thrown against
    space as if on a
        sinking ship, giving absolutely
everything up to, with
    nothing held back,

our own psychic zoological garden, and

we ourselves in their
creaturely story as well, they also
strolling down an aisle in that
same train, greeting us, exchanging a
   glance through
     eyes that once saw
things totally differently, totally and
insanely committed to deep bonds through
     eternity, cut off in this

life and divided now into
separate segments, and there were no

rancor or attachment, only a
universal recognition of the
poignancy of each and everyone's
   mortality,

on a train, going through a
  landscape, snowy or
    full of sunlight, going

    nowhere in
     particular.

2

The train we're on actually
  turns itself inside-out inside each
    one of us, so that its

compartmentalized trajectory rises up inside
  us, the outer visitations and sweet
    exchanges become plant growths of
psychic resonance that continue
    thriving in colored shadow long after the
real flesh encounters have
      bleached to black and white.
Our bodies become the train,
sitting relaxed, arms at sides, legs
  crossed or side by side, in
a jumbled chronology, in which the
    last might be the
      first, the first
last, all those
  people looking out of
    windows, taking
    coffee in
  pure white cups. Mountains and clouds and
    streams flowing
      by.

All those
various people with their
variable characteristics and combinations of absolute qualities
making up one giant composite human being which we in our
individualized separateness actually
reflect, and that reflection is in itself

the reflection of divine qualities so sublimely abstract it's as if
each one emanated from a creamy
star sapphire amphora perched on a

    special palisade with blowing dark green
        cypresses behind it,

each person with whom we've ever
  meshed is an opening in
    space from God's
      direct Names and Attributes
like so many billions of invisible birds flying down at
terrific velocities to make up the
  branching character of each person of us

spreading its giant limbs and leaves for the birds to
    land on out from our

central-most cores.

                                              12/28-29

SLEEP TWIST

I turn slowly in bed
  like a man drifting through algae,
    my erotic palladium in muffled uproar,
twisting bodily, and mentally entwined,
      to find the outlet.

To find the surface of sunlight,
rise up to the
world's sunlight bathing all horizontals and
shapely protuberances equally, warming
a reptile's body to pure endurance, our bodies to
something akin to love. It's
that easy. Theoretically.

But here in the tunnel of my bed, solitary, as
  solitary on the iceberg of
    momentary existence as a
cold blue ray, nowhere to
go, walls protect me against the
  rampage of disintegration possible and even
    inevitable in the
world of matter, matter itself

holds me as protectively as a
  German nanny, and the

fantasy kelp that keeps me in thrall also
wraps me, swaddles me like a
live mummy.

1/9

TO BE COMPLETELY OPEN

If a person could be so utterly and totally
    exposed as to be
completely open, nothing obscured by
   shadow or
      subterfuge, no
pretense or double-face or
      double-talk, our
persons so blindingly
    exposed to the light of
      divine scrutiny, walking
forward to meet the high-pitched
   hum with
no more mirrors and special effects, no more
long banyan leaves cunningly
   arched across to
      cover us, those
    soft black antelope eyes of
fear and awe fixed outwardly on
      anyone noticing,

we would be like high noon,
we would be like a room in a
   high castle suddenly thrown
         open to public inspection, we would
resonate the way every
twig and twig-beetle resonates in a
      rainforest during a sudden
          downpour,

our chambers would be thrown open, the nearest
lake or large body of water would be
bathed in the same light as the
landscape of ourselves completely opened,

nor would this exposure mean our death, the
   putting to death of all the
     lovely ambiguity of being
       alive, rather it would
link us up indelibly with all creation's
most arcane secrets, as
ambiguous as the
   blind mole or all-seeing
eagle in flight, our

sitting on a high mountain as much in
repose as our sitting surrounded by the
honking of human traffic, on a
   street or in a room filled with
people, our
   resources and impulses the
     same in both
   cases, the same as the

sounding of a
monumentally large bronze bell
as well as its

silence.

1/9

USED BOOK STORE OWNER

In memoriam Sally Blaufuss

I imagine when she goes home after
   locking the old store for the night, after
all day surrounded by bags of dusty books and
  leaping dusty cats, looking up at
    customers with tattered
      treasures under their
    arms, both
      coming and going,

she locks the front door, all the cats
    fed, litter box clean,
goes home to her pet crow, lies
   down on her bed, and all at once

a new landscape surrounds her, arctic
   jags of glacier blue as topaz glitter with
      the light of endless day,
she drifts onto the black waters of a
      lake, lines of seabirds
  drawn straight in the sky above her, the
    bed with her form on it
      turns in the current, light
rays down at golden diagonals to guide her into

now dense tropical estuaries, profiles of
   the great authors of her days pass in
      fragile outline in the

air above her bed, their
raspy, whispering voices repeating the
    lines and lines of words that
    wreathe around her all day, now

arching in the air of her night,
slowly turning in her dark room,

creatures taking refuge in the shadow of her form,
words holding her up like springs,

pale otherworldly light like gentle verbs
    playing across the nouns of her
        face and eyelids.

                                                1/15

THE PUZZLE AT PRESENT

1

Writing into darkness. Plans. Xeroxes.
  Drafts and maps. A grand structure
    o'erarching all.

Dovecotes. Into which even
  The Dead Sea Scrolls might find
both refuge and conduit into the
    light of day.
Honeycomb. Replicates those
  celestial interstices in the
      mind.

The penster, old hatted and ankle-length cloaked,
scrunched over teak wood desk in an
  afternoon of the world so late
    even blooms have
      begun their silken descents.
Light on the ocean there, between
  water and sky, has turned into a
    single russet thread.

The chronicler, hunched over blind
   writing in the dark, sees
glowworm-like apparitions appear between
   checkerboard patterns in
     space enough to imagine
emissaries could enter from a subtler world

to enlighten us. Our scribbler
   looks sharp. His eyes
     burn holes on the
       fresh white sheet so
well do they focus the incandescent
   sunlight of his
      intent. For he is

more than a wielder of pens — the
   geysers and cataracts of our
     earth culminate in his
       form. Sitting
bent over in his
   high chair over a
     long table
you might not see the teams of galloping white
   horses in his
     blood.
Architecturally accurate
  plans bleeding out from his
    spread fingertips.

Bridges of imagery lacing together
   disjunct worlds.

The night that covers us
     worn at an
oblique angle on the
   back of his

   worshipful head.

2

For it's all worship, my darlings —
   key in a lock, and the
      first footfall over a threshold —

a skylark scribbling its signature in flight,
a hard nut hurtling groundward —

Hard and soft textures sing His praises.
Lambs huddle inside morning pens,
white mist low over green gorse,
rough rock jutting from shale,
a child sitting still in long shade,
wild trees in formation down a steep hill
    to a raw sea.

It's all worship, my beauties,
  your hands at your sides, faces
    naked above throats,
small animals wrestling in warrens,
moonlight aslant across cactus,
  wasps pausing in midair,
    snakes sipping moisture
      through hollow tongues —

I get the stories wrong, dear hearts,
  forget the punch lines or
    leave out essential bits,
but their essences float in bubbles in space
  reflecting the Other World's light

on their round sides
   floating above cut lawns and
      peaked roofs —
entering rainbow-ribbed invisible forests of
   velvet shadow cast by
      any material object, *it's*

   that close!

The universe opens and closes like a silken accordion,
cascades pour down its wheezing sides
   into green pools,
  hummingbirds dart through
    watery strands to bathe and
      hover for a microsecond as
hard drops hit incandescent green
   wings and
     tiny blue heads.

Praises pour up into the sky from
wide open mouths of earth,
each hoof-clop, ant-tread, spider-tick of legs,

each thought in its gossamer threads, each
bite of predator, submission of
  victim on dusty plain, each

dawn over a battlefield illuminating the
   haphazardly scattered slain

is difficult worship of

    God's power

seen from inside our
   fleshy nutshell, all
     planets and stars
envisioned from between warm lids
   inside our miniature
     imaginary metropolis
   on two legs or less,
seated or standing, lying in
    sleep or half-waking,

each word of us fully equipped for
   flight to unknown spaces,

each thought of us
a thunderclap over Kansas,
a medicinal plant opening sticky pods in a rainforest,
a screech of iron streetcar wheels in Moscow,
a light in a test tube in alchemical laboratories,
a soft hand folded in a soft hand
   in the shade of a golden wall
     on a windy mountaintop,

the silence of a newborn after
such apocalyptic commotion.

3

I sit at a table in Philadelphia,

    a kitchen table in a row house in Philadelphia with
authentic Flamenco music in stereo from my
    Walkman through left and right headphones making that
3-dimensional dimension open up in my head of that
night spent in Cordoba once at an
all night Cante Hondo concert where
three or four singers sitting in chairs on a platform
sang one after another to one or two
 guitarists, and they
   hurled their longing into
    the night until pale pink sunrise,

and I was going to begin this poem
*"I sit at a table in Philadelphia overlooking
   the ruins of my life,"* when

my life is hardly in ruins, although a
   deep and real part of me is,

piles of dust and a stark blast of white
sunlight beating down on wind-blown foundations — *Ha!*

And a dazed, bedraggled figure in
too big clothes
staggers out waving loose arms at an
  imagined moon, twists in grinning
    circles between two
      giant iguanas who
  never blink — they blend in with the
    slate black night —
he sings: *"The matchsticks have burnt down to the*

blistered thumb that holds them.

*The rose's mane of petals doesn't
make it a lion.*

*Four loves in one life is equal to the
taking of tropical territory by force*

*where the natives
make you king!"*

The ruins of his life begin slowly coming together like
flakes, separate in distant places. They
   pick themselves up, they themselves
     long to be rejoined, they themselves

make the long trip on dusty feet
to reunite with the parts that will make them
   whole. Tent-flaps, reflections in
     quicksilver, a face, part of a face, a
  smell of hair, smell of sweat on a certain afternoon,
     apricots, taste and smell of them
        both, their
     sticky juice, these

elements like so many threads wriggling by their
own volition, like
   jumping beans under a
     heat lamp — loves unforgiven,
hatreds unrealized, angers
   unmodulated, speeches unmodified,

bits and pieces of a broken life, alas,
like sperm heading luminous toward the
egg that will suddenly begin a slow spin into
a body of new being, so that when heaven's

particular slant of light burns down into that
secret womb, arms and legs twitch, eyelids
snap open for an instant in assent,
the heart beats, the sex tingles,
toes flex, the whole head tilts...

I call invisible legions to my sides,
a woman's voice in my right headphone says
   something in Spanish above the
      clicking of castanets and
         strumming of strings,

"Forget the ruins of your life," she says,

*"we're all parts put together at the last
  instant after lives lived in*

*haste and understood backwards as the
 pinpoint goes through the page*

just as it gets turned over." —

That blank page following

is all our hope.

4

> *Man is a little cosmos —*
> *the cosmos is a big man.*
> — Sufi saying

Of course, I said, I could
   write anything. I
put a stepladder right up against the
   sharp edge of the night and
  climbed up to get
    closer to the stars.

I threw the shadow of a large moose on the ground.
There was no wind. I
   flapped my arms.
Kansas flapped. Fields fainted. Heads bowed,
   cornstalks prayed.

The spray from lawn-sprinklers spun rainbow halos
   in the noon.

Here's the catch. I got
   down from the ladder
and the trap door fell closed against the
  organ sound rumbling under the
    mountain.

The covers came down over most of the
  planets, out in their own
    atmospheric pools with frayed

    debris floating around them.

But the real catch is: The seasons
stopped to take a rest. Winter
warmed up by the hearth of the heart,
Spring idly, and humming to itself,
   strung pearls across black windows,
Summer lay in a hammock wasting its life,
Fall steadied itself through a flutter of brown leaves.

It all came round full circle,
but by that time we had all
passed on, the great ones whose
   fame lit up their steps long after
fleshed bone resounded against asphalt,
the anonymous with their faces of newspaper photographs,
all of us
   packed up a few things and boarded the
fiery bus. We

waved goodbye. But since
   everyone alive was on the same bus
there was no one to wave to, no one to
mark the impact of the
   poignancy of that single
     immortal gesture.

5

I get up and move to the railing

   across a room of glass floors, potted
     palms, murals in motion, and
gaze out across breakers under a tropical sundown.

I turn from the
railing to see the empress in brocade so thick
   you might imagine spontaneous
     creation taking place in its twists and deeps.
She glides across the floor in velvet slippers, her
  smile enigmatic and uncertain. Her
eyes have in them
    the knots of secrecy, the glaze of deception, and the
eruptions of Philippine volcanos too long
     dormant.

I turn from the
railing and see the room's walls tremble, they
  open up and behind their
    theatrical screens lie expanses of
      planetary motions, lumps of
    orbs through clouds, each with a
distinct atmosphere uniquely capable of supporting
  uniquely different life-forms, gargoyles of
    blue transparency on one, ferns of
      borealis silk leeching across a
        red ground cover of gelatinous
  ooze — on one planet
different colored smoke, on another
    rainbow-colored ice.
The planets' rounded bulks
      can be seen

rolling at different rates, rivers or earth-ruts
goldenly visible before
    dipping below an
        horizon of blue fog.

The empress of the second stanza appeared between these
orbs walking slowly toward me, her gaze
   averted. She
opened her arms wide and
    out flew flamingos.

I get up and move across the
   usual floor confronted by the
     same daily tasks of
       food intake, gratitude,
     expectation of
       ecstasy, forgiveness and
withdrawal from materiality. The room
   cleared of bric-a-brac, the
     head cleared of
       cheating thoughts, betrayals,
the heart on its knees before the
waterfall that never ceases falling.

Beyond the railing —
the waterfall that
never ceases falling.

6

That
   waterfall that
     never ceases falling has all our
   praise. We glimpse it from the
      side and it
looks like the world. When we
   look at it straight on
     it has the face of an angel.
Glisten of water-strands, coil of spray-ropes,
   web of wetness, downfall of
      giants to drops, light

shredded into
   cascade-lines hurtling to the
      rocks below, a supersonic
downward comb of liquid in which
   light is braided into
     small rainbows like
      half-moon discs that
leap out the sides into
      thin air.

That
   waterfall that
never ceases falling has in it
   our prayers, our
     eyelids saying their
       beads, our
heartbeats saying their

    silences between beats in which whole
worlds come to birth in the
      glint-edged wings of a
single dragonfly darting through the
    shaved rainbow and into the

waterfall that

never ceases

falling.

7

When I contemplate my
  terminal illness —
(I have a pain in my
   kidneys today so I
     imagine cancer of the
      kidneys and
 what would I do if I had only a
   few years or less to live?)
What would I do with that precious time allotted me?

Famous old question we've
  all asked ourselves.

Would I take a long walk, a long, long
   walk through the
     prairies and midwest cornfields

stopping at diners and
    talking to everyone over
  homemade pie and
    wretched coffee, connecting by
eye and voice to those
  middle Americans so rarely seen or
      heard from? Then

take off down the road, getting
    extraordinary energy for the trek by the
      fact of my
        terminal illness. Always my

back to everyone, facing the
  sunset, down the
    long road to the
      dark horizon?

Or would I spend all those last days on my
  knees, going over
    every last
      detail and
asking forgiveness? Look searchingly into
    everyone's eyes for the
answer to my
    supplications? Would I

go on talk shows telling of my
    terminal illness and asking to read
some poems, trying to get the mainstream interested in the
  touching, tender moments, the

      irascible, outraged moments, the
vital perceptions and kaleidoscopic visions available
   in poems, the human
      heartbeat and breath sauntering
freely through the
    rhythms of words to a
      total nudity of
        soul in the complete
    generous austerity of God's endless creational Light.

Now that would be an adventure worth
   going on! And why couldn't I
   do that now? Am I
     not really convinced of the
terminalness of my
    illness? The hiss and again hiss of
the snake-clock that
   strikes and
    strikes again at the
     exposed vein in our
   hearts, the moment slicing
clean through any illusion of
    endlessness, this

full-color moment sitting at the
   dining room table writing this while
wife and daughter banter upstairs and the
    refrigerator hums. I would

go to Tunisia to sit near a saint to
   remember in my

  deepest core what true
    sainthood's all about. Perhaps
then I could die of my
   terminal illness,

the pale hand pulled out of the glove, the

dark fire gone out.

8

The roaring ferocious lions of dream
  clamber up from of the pits of consciousness
to become flimsy paper cut-out kittens of themselves.

The tropical tornados of dream
  with houses arching on the backs of tidal waves
   and screams writhing like pythons between
     palm trees
become an echoing light breeze
  wafting across an awakening cheek.

The Art Deco multi-colored metropolis
   of dream with its giant nuclear drum
    turning at the horizon, its
  flying cars and heliports, Tanya in
   green spandex, Sage Kroppin with his
    fiery blue head and voice like
     clanging metal
ripples to the surface of consciousness like a faded

    postcard of downtown Minneapolis

and where do they go? Why have their
   fragile presences made us
     sweat or cry out, but when we
awaken they are curled wallpaper vaporizing the walls of
   a disappearing house?

Just as we, having crossed the obstacle course
of our lives lengthwise to the
   Next World will wake up, and all these
  tumbling traumas will be only
     the squeaks and whinings of a
       distant ectoplasmic tricycle that
wobbles off, riderless, down a
hill into a flat vast ocean of pure quicksilver where
all dreams must go to get

melted down to their vaporous essences
at last.

9

There is virtually no representation possible
   of anything
     by word or image,
lightning slash of color, scream, or silent gesture:
Everything represents only itself. Which is saying:
Everything represents the Holy Pronoun of
   Absence. Tunnel

flat as the air we breathe

down which we go

toward a spherical light

over an octagonal sea.

                                                         1/15-2/15

GETTING DRESSED

Solitary in a room, naked as a
   young bird, he pulls on
socks of river silt, their flexible brown
  ribbing pulled high along his shins,
puts one leg in shorts white as snow, moths
   flitter around the weave, dart
     in and out of a darkness made
       palpable by shape when they
take his human shape of squashed rump on flat bed —

over his head and down
  comes the undershirt of
dry waterfall from an indistinguishable height,
drifting down across shoulders and chest,
tucked at the stomach into snug fit of shorts —

Then the shirt. Now the shirt of
   stag-breath misty in the morning,
     doe acquiescence of alert breathing:
First the right arm's tube pulled straight along an
   akimbo arm to the armpit
     where one blind mole sticks out its snout,
then the left arm ditto, mirror-image to the right —
buttoned, with click-sound of water drops on
    dry bamboo all down the front, also
     ready to be tucked at midriff point
into trousers pulled from feet to waist,
tunnels in which anything germane to long
   darkness may dwell, tunnels of

    love for long-distance walkers,
   tunnels of fortuitous encounters, those
hairy legs of his stretch out like
     momentary pontoons across brackish
       Philippine backwaters and
the trousers are pulled from their
   holes to the unfurling of black fabric
to his waist, meeting-point of
   west winds and eastern cavalcades,
the waist below
  belly-button above
    crotch, belted now, like a
lithe highway-flattened snake come alive
     just in time to clamp its
       tail in its teeth, snapped
shut, he
adjusts his trouser waist with both hands,
he adjusts the tuck of shirt-tail into waist-band,

he stands up in the bedroom window's blue
    sunlight and
  strides out the room.

His two shoes stand at attention by the door.

He walks past them.

He
needs to die
barefoot.

2/27

LIFE AND DEATH

1

Death let down its black hair
Death sat hard on a cold slab

Life brought suit
Life displayed its silverware

Death had some blueberries
Death sighted a stag on a snowy hill

Life said *"adios"* into a napkin
Life looked at the page for a long time

Death drove a tricycle through the flames
Death opened the next-to-last drawer

Life paled at the thought
Life punched a blue ticket

Death drooled from its mouth
Death shed a green tear

Life opened its shirt
Life suggested another interpretation

Death had a gray piece of the puzzle
Death sat up straight in its chair

Life said *"bonjour"* into the bouquet
Life looked sad then happy

Death got comfortable
Death stayed in an awkward posture for a long time

Life embraced the lost orphan
Life sent the sweepstakes certificate to Sweden

2

Death shaved ice
Death wore a poppy collar

Life drew roses on a white sheet
Life embroidered scallop-shaped cloth

Death wore a large toupee
Death drank vinegar

Life put ice in a glass
Life wrote a long letter

Death saved its biggest surprise for last
Death sawed off a limb

Life drove wildly
Life savored the last drop

Death saved the last drop for itself

Death sounded the horn

Life sat under a large tree
Life spread its utensils on a cloth

Death played chess with a Chinese race car driver
Death hoped we would all keep quiet

Life tried to hide its affairs
Life always tipped its hand

Death neither stripped away nor covered over
Death left things as they were

Life tried to start trouble
Life went big-screen

Death sky-dove successfully
Death could count clouds all day

Life looked at its bank account
Life pulled out

Death spoke in a whisper
Death had a stage voice

Life spoke in complete sentences
Life followed the rules of grammar

Death rode a white palomino in the parade
Death turned on the lost faucet

Life scoured the horizon
Life saw the handwriting on the wall

3

Death is a lake turned to silver foil
Death is a hairbrush full of weeds

Life is a sock-drawer on fire
Life is a closet full of bats

Death is a shoe on a blue sidewalk
Death is a cobweb made of toothpicks

Life is a grocery store full of frogs
Life is an envelope with one side torn

Death is the shadow of a fast bicycle
Death is a whinny from the last stall

Life is a stroke and a strike and is struck
Life is a button on a stuffed millionaire

Death splashes cold water on the deck
Death is a calendar made of glass

Life dips and dives and disappears
Life is a Frigidaire humming on a back porch

Death is a shadow under a house
Death is a back stairs full of reindeer

4

Life wears a skullcap
Life wears loose shoes

Death looks at itself in a mirror
Death climbs a yellow ladder

Life scoffs at quitters
Life slouches in dark doorways

Death is sweeter than a summer's day
Death sticks a rock-tip into blue soup

Life snickers when the fat man falls
Life swaps leather for wood

Death synchronizes its watch
Death sits in the same place every day

Life walks slowly past the park
Life isn't interested in the details of the divorce

Death sends its hair and nails in to be analyzed
Death slips down an iron shaft

Life left its hat on a bus

Life threw kisses at the majorettes

Death sank to its knees inside the taxi
Death squirted orange liquid out of a gun

Life swept the floor and went away
Life swang back and forth with its feet raised

Death couldn't wait for the light to change
Death waited for the light to change

Life left its gloves at the funeral parlor
Life flipped the pages of the glued magazine

Death closed down the shopping mall
Death told her fortune using small sticks

Life left chicken bones on a plate
Life pushed back its chair

Death lifted its hat in deference
Death touched the shoulders of the judge

Life saw angels in a tree
Life watched the grass bend

5

Death wears rouge
Death wears a glass slipper

Life has a sprig
Life lets its thoughts wander

Death rides a steamroller
Death sideswipes a cavalcade

Life lets its propellers spin
Life warned us about the scaffolding

Death had a dark toothbrush
Death enjoyed joy rides

Life said hello to the mailman
Life brushed past the movie star

Death kept things in a cedar trunk
Death relaxed in a musty attic

Life careened drunkenly around a curve
Life said hello to the undertaker

Death said hello to the mailman
Death accommodated itself to the cramped conditions

Life sailed on a smooth sea
Life packed all its trinkets

Death paled at the thought
Death said its farewells to the assembled crowd

Life hung impressionist paintings in the atrium

Life squinted through tinted glasses

Death favored its one good eye
Death wore face makeup

Life latched onto the littlest bit of news
Life contorted in front of a mirror

Death shelled pistachios
Death savored the moment in silence

Life appreciated the sudden silence
Life sat for a while alone

6

Death broke rank
Death slapped the barrister

Life swayed back and forth
Life laughed out loud

Death smeared the rayon
Death sliced the tomato

Life shouted in an empty subway
Life hurtled past the barricade

Death broke the sound barrier with a boom
Death snapped the scissors

Life leaped across the chasm
Life split the log in two

Death rolled down the steep hill
Death pulled back its lips from its blue gums

Life stuck out its tongue
Life tried on the gauze wings

Death swooped out of the sky
Death latched its hook onto the pulley

Life threw the bucket down the well
Life ran across the field naked

Death tore the shirt off the minister
Death sawed through the last slat

Life leapt across the tracks just in time
Life swore under its breath

Death placated the bereaved gypsy
Death softened the blow

Life pulled its punches
Life cut through the last cable

Death swallowed the big pill
Death held its head under the faucet

Life caught the falling child

Life laughed as it went over the falls

Death caught a terrible cold
Death put gold leaf on the bare boards

Life sanctioned the parade
Life left the manhole covers open at night

7

Death waited for no man
Death sat in the steam bath
Death hacked at the lavish head
Death sent out for beers
Death rolled up to the front door
Death seated itself opposite the soprano
Death tried on elbow-length gloves
Death set its scooter under the stairs
Death said nothing worth repeating
Death saw the shaft of sunlight and swooned
Death, rage against inconsequence!
Death, salute the last straw!
Death, sit up straight and take it like a man!
Death, don't debate the results before sleeping!
Death, let the little ones go!
Death, let your rattles syncopate!
Death, lift your drawbridge!
Death, bat an eye!
Death, swat the opposition!
Death, let the old ones over the line!

Death, display your underarms!
Death, salivate in Technicolor!
Death, take the best ones last!
Death, let the lace fall slowly!
Death, shit on the moon!
Death pistols of pastewax!
Death calliopes in deft syncopation!
Death understated and underrated!
Death overestimated and slowly originated!
Death sprocket lock!
Death knows no adversary

8

Life sat patiently while the waters receded
Life lifted its eyeshade and focused its squint
Life forced its way in
Life foresaw the collapse of the north wing
Life slopped the wallpaper paste onto the dog
Life mattered to the car mechanic
Life barreled through the supermarket
Life drew in its head
Life believed itself safe from harm
Life saw death out the rearview mirror and gunned the engine
Life beaded the loose beads tighter
Life screwed the little screws first
Life crossed swords with the archduke

9

Death opened Life's chemise
Life bent closer to inhale Death's perfume
Death wriggled out of Life's clothes
Life opened the windows to let Death's curtains flutter
Death let its smile show Life's teeth and tip of tongue
Life looked long with fluttering lids into Death's eyes
Death stood on the bridge with arms around Life's waist
Life licked its lips as it fumbled with Death's zipper
Death opened the sheets to blinding whiteness as Life lay back
Life opened its eyes and closed them, feeling Death's breath
Death moved close and lay full length along Life's long limbs
Life pushed a sock off with one foot, then the other sock
   with the other foot, in Death's close embrace
Death cradled Life's head in warm hands
Life pushed its tongue deep into Death's mouth and ran it along
   Death's teeth
Death covered Life's form with congenial curves and gradual
   movements
Life pushed forward, lifting one leg against Death's weight
Death entered Life in a smooth silkiness and trembled
Life saw the window fill with Death's light
Death shook the furniture and exploded inside Life's body
Life moved around Death with slow melodious movements
Death glanced at the birds out Life's windows fluttering away
Life saw light billow across Death's sky
Death closed its eyes in a last throb of Life's energy
Life closed its eyes around Death's cool darkness

3/13-21

IN MEMORIAM DAVID RATTRAY 1937-1993

Attempting the improbable, he achieved the
  indescribable:
Bare moose-head burst through a wall.

Attempting the incalculable, he reached the
  indecipherable:
O hidden stairway, I love you
    past starlight.

Never settling for the purely mundane, he
  resembled the restless alchemist:
Brute force drove the green wedge through the
    iced rock.

Surprised by the energy, he chose the
  subtle way to soul-growth:
Blue light flashed radiance out
    from under gulls' wings.

Seeking the invisible, he became invincible:
Rank upon rank of peacock-tailed angels
    ringing in giant orbits.

Reaching for the unquenchable, he drank the ineffable:
Sing for the neon grape and call out for
    sweet raspberry.

Eyeing the furtive profile, he found himself
  face to face with the sky's countenance:

Heads of green light stutter forward out of a niche.

Led by a hunch, he pursued cosmic law:
Dust-motes fall in a spiral pattern through a
    sun-shaft.

Attracted by honey, he became a drunken pollinator:
God's great gardens
    never boasted so many roses.

3/26

ANOTHER DAY

1

Another day, another perfect crystal
   bead added to the row, another
day further from childhood and
     another day closer to death, another
four-dimensional collection of moments freeze-framed
    and set in blue ice on a
      fiery mountaintop in Tibet,

another white horse taken by the halter down a
   green slope, another
phone ringing in an iron box under the saint's
   tree, another
circle of birds listening to wisdom from the
     beak of an egret —

the twelve steps and ten doors and three main
   corridors and seven rooms
     looking out onto the hanging gardens
traversed in one day! Winks exchanged, words
well or badly managed, hearts
   touched or left untouched in the
      commerce of every day, even with
   people who are
      closest to you — the Veil of the Mysteries falls

perpendicular and firm against our ever really

knowing our reality in this world except in the

silhouette we ourselves cast against a wall of blue darkness,
the subtle motions we ourselves make in a
    forest of cool stillness,
a call looped out from our upturned
    hearts like earthen jugs with round mouths open under
        wolfish moonlight —

the soul's longing like lengths of our
    vision of existence getting
        shorter and shorter with
    each day, day after
        day —

another
wisp of white smoke above a
scented heap of rose ash.

2

Or another day, after that
    first day of the poem — this is
        the next day — walking around all day
like a flat-faced brownstone building looking
    out on an empty street with
brick steps going up to a blocked doorway —
    gradually the sun lifted, the
        light lifted its visor and shone
            blast of gray beams onto the

      wall, little by
little my eyes growing
accustomed to the light so I could read the
handwriting on that wall, that said:
*"You turn yourself inside out
and never know what to expect,
one day the people are like
   rose trees whose
      faces are melodious clocks,
the next day a doorknob's on fire, the
     street is thin ice, the
stairways are all descending."*

So that
   this day is all
      gnarled straitjackets untwisting,
police horses standing by iron grilles and neighing,
another day of men from Borneo standing around naked in
early morning drizzle comparing nightmares and
     laughing lightly in a gray fog —

black butterflies rise out of marsh grass,
triangular windows open in the blue,
another day shuffling forward on beaver feet,
another day of flip-top clip cap snapped
    open then clicked
       shut.

3

Or another offshoot off the day
   Cleopatra barged down the Nile,
      Anthony hot in his armor in Egyptian humidity,
         enduring all for her sake,
another day, this one, Philadelphia April 1st,
extension off that day, or off
the day the wise cobbler looked into the pewter mirror on his
         mantle and saw
rows of angels from his
   fingertips to God's Throne and sighed,

another day, this one,
another streetcar in Stuttgart, another
   barnyard full of rusted machinery, another
gold toothpick off the King's table, another
billow of factory smoke across a
   perfect Byronic landscape,
another day, utterly
     unique — I

lie in my bed at one-thirty in the
   morning tallying up the Spenglerian
evidence for the
     Decline of the West, doorknobs
        fallen off into sparse grass,
whole grandstands full of cheering spectators
   collapsing like balsawood,

the bus pulls up and opens its door like a

    skull's grin, and out pile
the deformed and mutilated victims of official Third World
    terror and neglect —

another day on the planet,
another day of benign indifference —

but if you go further in you find
    Divine Interest in the
      minutest particular, and if you go in past
the minutest particular you find
extravagant blessings on the supra-molecular level,
microscopic banquets in the Great Hall of the
    chromosome, valleys of the
hungry suddenly bursting into green abundance,

the flutter of an eyelid, the huge
   black eyes on a sunken
    face illumined by those
rows of genuine angels the medieval
   cobbler saw, the same ones, and not a
second older,

ascending stairways like xylophone notes past the
telephone poles of
   terrestrial distances, singing —

another day, objects made of
   cloud, emotions made of
cloudstuff puffing away, dissolving in
   white fleecy

    brilliancy,

wisdom like the dripping of gold ingots into the
form of all of us watching
this day, another
    day like all the
  rest, pass
drop by drop into tomorrow, the
    2nd of April in
        Philadelphia, another

day altogether.

4

Or another day
   hosing off the tigers — we had
     gone to the zoo my
one day off this week, I exhausted from my
day job (my night job I
    put ladders up to stars, take a
      scouring cloth to the
  moon's face, bag
    small bulbous clouds with purple and gold
      linings for
        later use — but I haven't given up my
day job...)

me staggering around a cold Sunday like someone barely
recovered from a

nervous breakdown (wife, daughter, and
little baby my wife looks after wiggly in her
          pushchair) —

at one point I found myself
alone in the House of the Carnivores, on a
    cement bleacher against a wall facing the
       indoor tigers' cages, and there were

three huge tigers, overgrown
    house cats — overgrown, that is, as in a
Maurice Sendak nightmare — and a
      woman with
         blond hair in ponytail and
            khaki maintenance uniform
turned a powerful spray of water on the
floor and tiles of their cages to rinse off the
odoriferous tiger-piss and other
     detritus of confined tigerhood, meat-bits,
         snarl-spit, God-knows-what,

when suddenly she trains the spray on Mr. Tiger!
I'm expecting a cat reaction — instead he
    lies down, head poised high in obvious
        tiger-pleasure, opens his
           back legs, lets her spray
private tiger-parts and tiger belly, and wonderful rippling
    tiger-sides, throat, front paws,
        up and down she plays that
            hose for a
long, long time, he never

   flinching for a moment, that tiger-face so
      pleased, finally

he lumbers up and starts
   running through the three connected cages, sliding on
      slippery tiles, losing his
         footing, turning and
loping back through the small doors, then the
two she-tigers, less
  interested in the water up to now,
start running as well,
    chasing each other, finally one of them
  submits to a dousing, sits still and
     lets the spray splash,

and I see them at a huge waterfall in the wild, one
   standing under the cascade
     force of it first, getting that
dust out and flushing those
    fleas in the process, sunlight
    shuttlecocking through careening strands of
      descending water-crash onto the

stripes of black and golden glistening bodies of
happy tigers, as these were
momentarily, as I was, dazed, gazing at a
secret ritual at the zoo,
the Hosing-Off of the Tigers, one cold

   Sunday in
     Philadelphia.

                                             3/30-4/6

FULL MOON

Driving home tonight after work, late, the
  full moon was that
    Blakean strange gauzy
     orb in a brown domain of
  light around it in a
sea of black sky, a thin
cloud-blade drawn across it, the craters
   bearing their bluish pockmarks down on us,

and I thought
what if the moon, this
  wolfish moon, got
    stuck at the full
      forever?
Our dear emerald planet with its
  pale pearl moon in space
suddenly under full moon influence every
night of our lives! Phosphorous

fish might come up from the
   deeps and make
    star-patterns on the
     water-surface,
humans might become even more
  adept at lunacy, lunar
    weirdness become the
  norm. Would

our teeth grow

    tiny and sharp, our
        eyes ruby?
Would we do
odd things like no more
count on our fingers, but rather our
    eyelashes, or the
        interior icicles of a lunar
            landscape unseen by
any but ourselves?

The sea might grow either
   glassily calm or subject to
     fits of jaggedness and
       choppy crests, maelstroms and

cyclops-filled waterspouts, and
people might push out in
    silver canoes at all
   hours of the night to
     become one with that
magnetic disk of eternal whiteness suspended beckoningly
       in black night.

Would all our
    skin become really white, our
      eyes turn to topaz, our
tongues more glissando-like, our
   limbs longer and
lankier? Would animals
     cast even longer shadows as they
       roam the Afric plains?

Would the cool lunar calm we see in
Buddha's face become ours
   as naturally as
      moonlight on a
        windowsill, or
moonlight filling all our
   rooms at
      once? Hecate and her
        sisters seated around the
moon — would their
   crooning bedevil us?

Would we end up
longing for long midnights of utter moonless
darkness, then the tiny eyelash sliver moon of
     monthly renewal?

Driving along under the full of it tonight, I
   was glad for the
      waxing and waning of it

  and the waxing and waning of everything else
      just as it is.

Full one second, gone
   the next —

We can't bear too much
   fullness for too
      long. Even God's

light to be known must
have darkness. Even our own

hearts fail.

4/8

BASEBALL STADIUM EPIPHANY

At the moment I entered the baseball stadium
a huge crowd ovation went up

and I found myself imagining it was for me
and my latest poem, for a split second our

culture had shifted drastically and was
capable of cheering a poet and his poor tropes,

thrilled at the ultimate victory of words of light
over the sleep of the human species,

overjoyed and eager to cheer the exact image
   and the sudden ecstatic flight of the soul

      for the good of all.

4/24

I AM A STUBBORN MAN

I am a stubborn man, cried Melchizedek,
   and will write poems no one wants to
     hear until the alleyways are
        piled high with them, the forests of

nightmare with their
gnarled red twists of tree trunks like human viscera
clogged with these expostulations of joy and rage.

Clog up the oceans, plug the great waterways!
Words on fire sluggish as drunk bats, light as
    spring fireflies, words from somewhere just behind
that goatish man's form, come out in

   feathery spurts coiling before his
     face like those

cartoon balloons on Aztec murals, Chalam Balam,
    Choc-mol, Methuselah of language

        living on.

THE POET DIES

The poet dies and leaves his
   toothbrushes on his tombstone: The silver one he
 brushed his teeth with
    before writing his poems; the wooden one he
brushed his teeth with before
    reading them to anyone; the plastic one he
brushed his teeth with just to go out in public —

he also leaves his first and last pair of shoes,
the first pair huge with so much promise, the last pair
  tiny as booties because as he
    grew in stature he
      diminished in size —

he leaves his
mortgage agreement exquisitely folded in the
   shape of a little origami bungalow —

he leaves the pins and needles he was always on,
  ectoplasmic socks, day-glo maps, drafts of
   cities built entirely on bridges, plans of
    cities built of
  pure crystal, imaginary cities where all the poor are
happy and don't miss dinner —

he leaves tickets to games never attended and plays
   devised by his own mind in which he
    dies and leaves all these
      things on his tombstone, flat in the

grass, with the inscription:
   "If the fool would persist in his folly
   he would become wise" — William Blake,
     evoked at the last and
        as always in his life,

the lilting and limpid bittersweet soft
    English voice of Blake
ringing in the air over the poet's grave like an
    invisible Buddhist monastery about to
        take shape out of the mist.

He said his farewells to everyone, he gave his
   cap and bells to his children who
      won't need them (they've
        all gone into business),

he fed his cat one last time, who
    grinned as he
       disappeared, leaving his
        own grin afloat in the treetops — he left his
   rat coat folded neatly on his
      tombstone like someone just
        jumped off a high bridge,

he didn't jump, he sank down into the
ground of his grief like a stone,

he sits up underneath the ground now and
   sets about redecorating his tomb,

he gets up and goes over to the window which
    lets in no light, and
      opens it so it
lets in light and air, and the sound of
    honking traffic and the whirling
      songs of birds,

he sets about with hammer and nails, glass
    hammer, angelic nails spun out of
      thought-saliva,
builds a bedroom overlooking the river,
a study lined with all the books he
    had always intended to read,

he puts in a stairway going up to the
    ground floor where he
meets his loved one over and
    over along the
      curving bannister, and their
eyes lock, and their heads come
    together, and light
      fills his tomb, the poet's
tomb refulgent with light

articulated into rhythm'd words becoming the
    speech of someone dead for years who,

eager and flushed with new-found
    facility, sings.

5/7

BACK STAIRS

Oh the fools that climb the back stairs
and the fools who refuse to climb them,

tongues like sunken boats.
Where do we go from here?

I see them rising and falling, carrying bricks?
When they fall they enter the air and make

rings all the way to the horizon
like a pebble makes perfect round

   rings to the edge of a pond.

Through space, their silent cries audible
only to toads.

And the toads don't care.

When they blink the universe crashes
then comes back again.

They open their eyes, those yellow, yellow
    eyes.

What do I know? They go to where those
yellow, yellow eyes show the way.

5/18

THE WAIT

While I'm waiting a half hour for the
   next train, having missed the one I
walked like a startled ostrich to miss, through the
   gently rainy bright green May Philadelphia
10:30 a.m. streets to the station, past
    banks of irises both pale and bright,

I could sit here on the broken wooden
fleck-painted bench and write

the entire history of the world, heartbeat by
   heartbeat. The outcome and
    origin of all our
     striving, a loving eyewink at the right time, or the
flat of an oppressive hand against a
   bare baby buttock that started our
uprise or downfall through all the
    tangled years of our lives —

I could write prehistoric mud holes, futuristic vertigos —

The great ones on their deathbeds, some of them
   afraid and drooling,
    yellow eyes rolling in their
   dry heads as they watch death's angel
    bend close, blowing ever so slightly those
     unsightly misty blue breaths, *puff puff.*

Or else the deathbed scenarios of

   the ones who grow solemn — eternity fills their
      mouths with its light golden marbles, and
         each serene word comes out
            round.

I could sit here facing the parallel iron tracks in the rain and solve
in a flash
the inexorable mysteries of mathematics. Numbers
   never converge, they run on parallel tracks, disappear
      at last in the One. Appear again like
         slick acrobats, ready to do their
anti-gravitational turns —

I could sit on this bench and see in my mind's eye
    the start of all the
   biological processes that
     got me here,
the tiny illuminated radiolaria, fragile
gelatinous spokes of the determined wheel of
    light energized with the
same smooth music that keeps planets like
      Neptune in black space spinning —

I could, in the time left before the
   train comes, write the
history of history, as well as all
    literature and wisdom — that
     single dot of God-sent bright light that
burns through the pages of every book ever written,
every book opened and read, that white heat of
   spirit-force and the

      relentless forward movement of
         ingenious thought over the
        arid plains of
paper and ink into the
  torn breast of each reader —

I could decipher the
   equipoise mechanism of language, that
both sun and moon reflect on the tongue's moisture
and send burning and icy beams of love through every
communication, by dolphin, dog, or
     man, insect, mite or
       minister —

I could sit here and write all the
mortal nights and days left to us, the Titanics of
   civilizations sunk to the bottom, Utopias
     risen on stilts above the
       muck of despair and longing
only to topple through the rise of the human ego
    mushrooming in a perfect place with
      the usual blood-lust for
        "perfect power" —

I could unweave the mystical labyrinths of sex,
that coiled green drive that opens out
   velvety buds of lavender in which green
     neon snakes linger and strike,
coil and intercoil of slippery
   gleam-grease, flutterings and
  upturned spouts and

    inturned cisterns where
        a liquid like slick sound
      slithers over our
        bodies with its
          blue soap —

Or I could resolve all the tragedies of love, have
    Romeo and Juliet not die, but
      open their slow eyes in that
        cobwebby crypt and glance
over to each other from their
   biers and their
     eyes fill with
        tears and their
mouths make sounds only
      their own ears
         hear.

Ecstasies and contemplative loop-the-loops. The vast and cratered
    history of the heart.

Bodily farewells and the souls' entertainments. Lying back and
     basking in
   God's Light. Arrivals in full
     regalia, stark naked.

Samothrace, that headless statue, with white marble wings flung wide
    and her head miraculously
        on again, smiling.

The joy of God's encirclement.

The long glass trumpets of His
 Greeting. The
endless dunes of His breathy Silences
 throughout the worlds. God's Voice
 like a perfect word, ending in a
 Shout.

Everything and nothing. At the
 heart of all our
 befuddlement —

Zone opened suddenly, going
nowhere and everywhere, at once.

All this, as I sit here, in this
 ramshackle train-station (Tolstoy could have
 died here), rain
 glistening down in strings
 dangling in front of me,

twinkling on the
straight tracks, waiting here

 for the train.

5/20

PUZZLEMENTS

1

The perception of imperfection in the universe,
   imperfection of anything any time,
      is a disease of the mind.

But this does not mean
   an imperfection in the universe, for it is itself
      a perfect
mechanism by which our hearts, those perfect instruments
      of perception, appreciate
God's unerring perfection
by coming back to it out of the

   mind's dark labyrinth.

2

I have a face of full moon.
My eyes are two crescent moons turned
   downward.
My mouth a dead crater.

I am a riddle whose
   answer is forgiven even before it's
      committed.

Large golden peacocks land on my head and

    swing their long tail-feathers
back and forth like pendulums, chipping
       sparks off night's anvil.

Bottles clear as ice stand on an ice wall.

Boiling inside them are the
    gratuitous elements of our destinies
      poured out into arctic blood
that shimmers golden as it crawls down our
    bodies to the sun's ocean.
Their fingers become golden, their tips scarlet.

Nothing prevents a stealthy leopard with
   golden eyes from peering between
     leaves.

My huge round head is
   full of hungers.

Is there no lyre whose plucked string is
   pure enough to rouse the
     sleeping army inside its
     bloody barracks of denial?

Doves rustle on the roof, slapping and shuffling.

The night rolls back its eye.

                                5/24

THE NEW TOWN

There once was a suburban town so new it
   felt nostalgic for
traditions it never had.
So it started constructing ruins.
Half-built pillars of concrete with girder plinths on top
  in open fields, erected in such a
     way as to look
lost and abandoned by
time and human neglect.

They studied that special weathered look of ruins, their
eerie silences, their stark skeletal remains forcing
    tourists to
  wonder about their
ancient inhabitants, why they disappeared, where they
went, what they
    did there.

Slowly these resourceful townspeople had a
town with ruins scattered everywhere,
looming arches above supermarkets, parts of viaducts by
parking lots, Roman columns near housing developments,
crumbled
    circuses.

They built an ancient wall abutting the back of the modern
library, square stones
  worn down smooth
    in spots, some

tumbled to the ground.

They put round stone seats around tall trees,
   a few facades or old highways
trailing off into the woods, and they were
satisfied that their

town stretched back in time to
   antiquity, their
pulses quickened with
imagined genetic continuity as they
buttered their toast popped fresh out of
   shiny metal toasters while
gazing out their kitchenette windows
  past picket fences at the

  mud-colored coliseum, half its
    ancient walls gone, rising
fantastically in the
      early morning light.

6/2

THE ACT OF LOVE

Maybe it's impossible to describe
   the palpable joy we have in
      lovemaking,
it's a non-verbal plenitude, wordless
unpunctuated four-dimensionality, sacred
        shapeliness
   honored in time.

Re-enacted in language, it has the power to unhinge the
   mind through the heat of its
      imprudence, perhaps, or the
impossibility of imparting its
   inimitable taste.

Fingertips following the sculptural
   edges of leg or hip, softening at the
petal-touch of genitals, fingertips like
a braille-reader's, cogitating the
   knowledges found there
     with a mind of their own
in a cosmos of total silence.

Memory comes in with its velvet drapes to
   drift over our
     turning bodies, giving them
   momentary form as they
twist and twist in the folds, falling in a
   silence of weightlessness, though in

reality our flesh and bones of love have a
   buoyant but down-weighted gravity, even a
growing heaviness, as if we go
     through our warm bodies
       into the earth, through flesh and veins and
   organs and skeleton, burrowing
      under earth's fresh crust
into the dark fragrant loam of it, mud rising all around us
while still we roll on a seeming cliff of steel polished to
     mirror smoothness
the sun makes brighter with its
silvery whiteness.

What am I saying?

You bend to me, night,
  with your heavy breasts
     full of
       moon-milk.
You become erect, you
   pulsations of thought.

I'm swept into lakes of
green moonlight by the
   breaths of our
    originators
on that first bed of our life played out to now

like a writhing net.

6/10

MOCKINGBIRD

1

I'm in a strange static state that is
   vaguely pleasurable — it is
night, humid, summer-hot, there's a
mockingbird a few houses down out there on a
   TV antenna chanticleering his
     vocal territory as far as he
can, and as

   far as I'm concerned it's so
     rapturously beautiful, so
harmonically elegant, he can
   stay there all year, my
territory's been ceded to his
   monarchy of sound, his
     totally unembarrassed
     variations, that high-pitched

whistle he's doing now is
scepter to his throne room of roof-high
   starry summer night under whose
dome he so elementally assumes such
     royal proportions. Oh, now he's

making raspy figures, he's actually kind of
   sizzling, there doesn't seem to be
anything he won't try —

and in a melancholy way that's how
I feel tonight, I could become
monarch of the world, though I've just seen
Mussolini's lifeless, battered body hoisted
    upside-down in derision by his
        countrymen, hardly a fitting
end
for a monarch of the world...
(is the mockingbird actually whistling La Cucaracha out there?)
and I have no worldly ambitions in that
    direction —

at the same time, exhaustion-prone, I could
lie across my bed and slip
   into sleep, leave the
kitchen a mess and food uncovered
(that mockingbird doesn't care, he has only
  one thing on his mind),

(there are two of them, I hear it now,
    call and reply, really!
And a sudden back and forth to take your
   breath away for its
     incisive musicality, sharp-noted, quick-
      exchanged, valleys of
  notes jabbed out, first from one, same notes
   from the other, as if one was
just an echo of the first,
then a burst of
  notes and they're on their
    own again, surrounded by

artistic solitude in the night.)

I can't pull myself away to do
kitchen chores. I don't want to miss a
   note. Their
 presence is
   sacred.

I find I have spent the whole evening
mockingbird-listening.

2

I really don't want anything so much as the
   next poem, adventure fallen off from the
last — the last one went so far, then stopped.

The next one opens up that grate, looks
   down into that mine, goes
down dark newly-cut steps with its
  meager lamp. When it's

over it's over, it could be a
poem of magnificent cut glass, facets showing some deep
wound slashed in our lives, some deep
fissure even Phoenicians
   puzzled over,

or a cure from the Country of Sacred Cures,
rare odorous herb brought in "by chance" by a child,

    across a thicket of sharp brambles, none
        puncturing her
          rosy skin.

What interests me is what depths in a new poem might
    fall away onto another
level entirely, or reveal an entirely new
paleontological strata, fossils coming to life in dream wandering
    around again stark naked and
        willing to share
  millennial knowledges. The

world of nature is like this, stark naked under its
    textures, in constant
        shifts of brutal harmony and
soothing salves of rupture.

Rapture in going into the self's dark that has had a
spark struck at its entrance — it may light up
only a few of the
    heiroglyphics, but that's
        enough —

even our feet roll forward as if on ball-bearings
to go down inky corridors into
the central chamber.

3

Adorable oracle!

Mouth in the air. Voice with no
  body — no

    visible body. Mouth up against
the present
  pouring out syllables,

mouth up against glass wall,
flat lips pressing glass.

I don't see your larynx but I
hear your sound. Even in another

room, another
space-dimension, another
    age, your hair all

kelpy and long-stranded, entangling me.

4

Each of us has got
  angel wings all around us,
angel wings above us
    in the air above us,
blue upon blue and white upon white
crowding out the air, oxygenating
    everywhere. Multiplicity of

wings in fluttering motion around each

    tiny act of ours. Each

breath of ours cradled by angel-wings,
each eye-flick, each syllable of words
   spoken into the air
     buoyed up by wings. Each

word unspoken has
   invisible wings fanning slowly
     through them,

each turn of thought all the way out to each
   turn of leaf on a lake, *O wings*
     everywhere!

(Tonight there's a solitary sound of a
   single mockingbird
     whistling for reply, but the
night is silent.

There are
angel wings all around that
bird, and above and below
that silence.)

Breath, heartbeat, blood-pulse, nerve-jump,
   wings upon wings, continuous
     ripple of the whitest
  feathers you've
    never seen, never
      will see in

    this world.

Air cut out of air, a hole in
    nowhere — *wings!* They're

there. Clear
   springs. Moonlit
     springs which undercoil
everything. Every

rock, flat, round, smooth,
  up-thrust, down-punch, level of
    eye or voice,

there are angel wings all around us, all the
   time, around
     us.

There are
angel wings
all around us.

                                          6/12

AFTER THE END OF THE WORLD

When you get older you
   drop things, that's
     all.
When you get older your
thoughts get knots
   like air bubbles,
    names evaporate as if
      overload mixed 'em.
Don't worry — they say
  the 20th century is the
   century of sensory overload.

When you get older you're more
   desperate about your
    dreams if you think you
     won't live to fulfill them —
something like Gauguin's expatriation to
  tropical syphilis even begins to
    look good in
      some ways, or far better

fleeing to live in
wool robes and pointy yellow shoes among the
incense-filled rooms of the
  happy poor of Morocco.

When you get older you also submit to
  grumpier days and various
body-cramps, funny lumps and

    sore-points, the
energy becomes more
     fleecy, crag-faced,
   zigzagged, not
less, but less sustainable except over a
     short span.

When you get older the arcade lights flicker,
but under dunes of
  large white feathers glow rows of
    green lights so
     lovely almost all
regrets or frustrations are forgotten.

An amber stairway about the size of a
hummingbird's egg escalates up out of a
moment in which mortality and
immortality are clenched in the
fingers of one hand like a
telepathic interpreter of objects to the
one-time people connected to those
objects, and they

all lead back miraculously to an
archway'd garden surrounded by
   stone lions whose

watery roar is enough to
wake the dead and
set them on their
heels again as

athletically alive as
ever, as active as a
slow glow-worm making that
staggering
green light glow now above a

lower path.

7/1

THE PUZZLE POTENTIZED

1

Is it necessary to point out at this point
that the game is over, that
walls have been collapsed, maze-hedges in the
   King's winter garden have been
cut to the ground,
all the Rubic Cubes have clicked into the
   Final Solution for all of us,
the slate of the sky has been
    wiped clean,

yet
the thirst for adventure and the
  lotions of love like a
    balm to the aching body
are still in effect, put into
  practice at a
    touch or a wink — or the

sudden alighting onto a cactus-ear
of an eagle so giant its form actually
  shadows half a continent?

The Puzzle: That there is no puzzle?
No. Too easy.

The Puzzle: That her eyes open onto the
  opulence of panthers lying on their

      sides on green velvet
yet she remains
  unconvinced of the basically
    miraculous nature
      of all things?

The Puzzle: That we go away and
    never return?
We become a long blue chalk in a long box
  that's stopped writing?

We become a slim bell only we can ring
  although no one hears us? It's behind
    sliding glass, sheets of
      static water?

We become stone in a rushing stream. We catch the
sun's glisten.

Or is The Puzzle simply our very nakedness of being,
caught in the shadow of the bright red beast who
hovers over all families and all
  genetic channeling? The rose

does not result from the pairing of rhinos.

Time is relentless, scratching its
wrinkles into our faces and across our
hearts like an
unforgiving schoolteacher. There seems to be
  no justice, no

    appeal.

Is time The Puzzle? (Winked as he
      asked)...

2

As serious as I've ever been,
  to whom do I speak?
Cast out these islands of neon flesh?
Break up bread and
  cast it on the waters
for what goggle-eyed golden carp
    to consume?

The boat-builder, his craft cut from
   tree-shape of crotch and
    sway of main branch and
solid heft of trunk
sees people get in and ride off, through
   choppy waves, or out over
still waters.

The house-builder from ground zero up
all around empty space on yonder hillside
sees walls with doors and windows, attics,
  basements, floors, ceilings, then
people with utter confidence the

floors won't cave through or the
    roof fall on them
move in with all their fragile furniture and a
      canary
to live out the best days of their lives
    (especially weekends).

The poet is a lopped bard in a boneyard,
a tipped hat in a hatless crowd,
an empty stadium with the turf-controller
    controlling the turf.
But who's waiting to listen, take in the
  pill and drink the
    clear water transported from
      Original Spring, the Eternal
        Spring?

We're all patients here, in those
gowns split up the back, all our
  fannies showing — some to
greater advantage!

I sit in a heat wave with the fan on low
so as not to drown out the
    sizzle of these words coming over the
      wires to me
to my less than perfect receptor.

I want to receive. Pray to receive.

But after?

3

Here in a heat wave day by the side of a
   bright blue pool, sound of
watersplash as daughter and girlfriend's voices
   toodle and trill as they play
penny-toss in the pool, dibble-dabble, and

I, paunchy dad, by poolside on a
   white metal table, be-
dazzled by
"The Puzzle." Seems so
  foolish, can't let it
    go, The Puzzle, its

hedges and its bets, its
labyrinths and splashes, its
   penny-toss into the deeps —

humped over a notebook, paunched, parched in this
heat, not by
   Sahara-side in a whitewashed
room above Sufi-buzz of
   devotional chanting, not
in a cloud-surrounded tower made of
   incandescent stones, nor even
at the end of a long trek, skin flayed at my
  sides in hanging strips, my
    yells both Gorgonish and
     gorgeous still
echoing in the

high-walled sacrificial enclosure, but a

father in funny black bathing suit by the
   bright blue rectangle of a pool,
girls' voices bouncing against flickering
    pool-tiles, playing tricks,
      kicking up spray,

The Puzzle, the awful
puzzle, night and
    day!

4

"Of all the images I've created," said the
   man of straw, *"none is as compelling as the
    flaming bicycle."*

"Of all the figures I've conjured," said Death in his
   sooty cloak, *"none is as
    persuasive as a
      pale yellow ribbon rippling
all by itself above a
    body stretched out."*

"Of all the thoughts I've made public," said the
   policeman, *"none is as lugubrious as a
picket fence rising up on its main posts to batter
    a ramshackle house."*
"These are trivial," said the woman who lives in stone.

"There is nothing so
   cunning as a body of naked light taking its
     skin off to reveal
        a secret darkness. Nothing so
soulful."

The cat came up. She was hungry as usual.
"*Nothing you can imagine,*" she meowed, "*equals
   a bird on a branch
   becoming a flying fish
     in through the window to land in my
       bowl next to fresh water.*"

The Knife Man snickered. Thin as a blade.
Pointed toward us all. "*Nothing can compare,*" he
   jabbed, "*with my
     slit up silk, my parting of
      hair in midair, my
cutting silhouettes in the dark.*"

"*Imagery is fine,*" said Our Lady of Snails,
   "*but a long silence can be finer. A
     long glistening silence.*"

The broad boards creaked as a three-legged man in
   iron jackboots came in rotating like a wheel and
     sat down: "*Nothing can beat
a golden hill under sapphire
   sky with emerald moon and
     real deer grazing.*"

There was a wall, a silence. A wall, silence.

*"No image so fine as the
   last one whose echo
      outlines the invisible
         one to come,"* said

the flushed face of the wind, the

petulant face of a cloud, the

featureless face of rain straight down on a

hot summer's night.

5

Asked by my own self:
   *"What do you know...
      what do you
   really know?"* — a
hard question requiring real
   answers, and no
poetic funny-business.

I know we don't go into our graves to
rot and a blank metal of nothingness
closes down over us, I know that, but
   how do I know it? The soul, the lit
truth of our lives

   slips out of us and goes to be
     elsewhere, the way
four dimensions invade three dimensions by, say,
poking us out of nowhere on our
   breastbones with a
     sharp poke as if by a
   ghost-finger.

All this glorious hummingbird sky-bath of
intelligent extravagance and stillness cannot simply
carbonize like paper into a cindery clench and be
done. My evidence is that
we all go on in sunrise after sunrise after a
beloved one's death, we
put on our shoes and comb our hair and have
dreams without end for minutes or
 years on end: Behemoth with

  smiling face come to
 save us out of an abyss, legs in
   light bicycling at a
cliff's edge in a race with
  time and
    winning, or losing — but it's actually

human eyes tell us this Truth, eyes of love, eyes of
children, eyes of the dying, will they
go to a place where there'll be no more
  seeing? When
   all of life is really a
universal continuum of

    gigantic *seeing!*

We come out of a tight place of
  undifferentiated light into
wide rooms and sunlit valleys of
varied shine and shadow, green
hills, green walls, differentiated
light and shadow of skulls and knobs and noses and
roses becoming slowly drawn over a lifetime back into
undifferentiated light again, all our
agonized struggle gone, like a shout
that echoes in a dead-end street,

suddenly blooming into fields of golden wheat —

I have no evidence for this except
the saying of it. I have no proofs or
signed documents. But it is

not just anyone's guess, it is
more like bridges looking frail from a distance
  but made of
steel girders
     on closer inspection —

and around the girders' bases white

moths flutter and fly off,

cluster and dissipate.

6

The sharpness of razors, the tall thin greenness of grass,
the incessant growth of green grass in a wet
   climate, the long dryness of drought and the
     subsequent brownness,
the way fog bleaches everything out and gets
snagged in cypress branches along the California coast
sometime in the 1940's,
the love of the mother and the
   mysterious indifference of the father,
the nonchalant sensuality of the older brother,
the cruelty of that same older brother,
the unreachableness of the older brother who
   had animal magnetism for a time then
     stepped into his own world and left me
       alone, but I had
formed a harsh opinion of him and all he represented
   by then — surely
unjust and untrue, except to my
      teenage mind...

The way fog lifts leaving a clear space underneath,
some conical rock formations in the Southwest,
hard granite and shale in fantastic formations
   like raven castles and haunted
     ritual pinnacles —

I know colors and their eventual
   resolution into blackness or intensest light,
sounds, notes, symphonies and their eventual

resolution into silence.

I have known the love of the mother and the
    joy and giddiness of the mother and her
       innocent interest in my doings

and I have known the mysterious indifference
     of the father and the
apparent fear of involvement, the rejection of
any interest in me, the insistent and fortified
    ignorance of my world and its thoughts and
        desires,

my father who is now in no grave, but whose
ashes were drifted over the Pacific one
foggy morning, though it may have been
   clear, and my
mother who is addled but alive and who
wants her ashes similarly strewn so as not to
occupy a grave we could visit and
talk to, they want to be
  gone with the wind and
     mixed with the wind and waters

and I know it is a strange request,
it is a myth of disintegration of the past with no
linkage to the unknowable future
that cuts the living off from the dead and makes the
dead not to care any more for the
living after their death, to be
   disposed of like a dustpan full of

  dust, thrown out.

I know no genetic connection with my
own family except what I
carry in my body, what's
circulating around in my
 daughter's body, and could
  go out into the world again
   through her,

but there is no way backward,
there is no visible trail back that
anyone can take in my line.

One feels a certain loneliness

that is a low dome of storms.

7

When the question's posed: *What do you know?*
 What do you
  really know?"
the blank Buddha comes along and
 kicks you into a stream. You
  drown.

You can't say, *"I know*
 this, I know that." You can't even say,
"I know God." Flamingos

    perch through the blanks.

Buffalo roam.
There's no one home.
It all gets outta' hand.

Monumentality shrinks —
  what's miniature gets

elephantiasis. Words fail.

Then those dumbfounding paradoxes flourish. Koans.
Sufi stories.
Improbable exclamations. You're

    beside yourself.

      With joy.

8

If, as I suspect is true for most of us,
what we don't know could fill tome after tome and
  dusty half-ruined Babylonian library after
    library with long moaning
      corridors repeating in triplicate all the
things we don't know, we really don't know, and

all the things we do know could be
written on the flap of a single matchbook,

from the variable slant of light at a
precise spot at the
edge of a forest all day to its
point of departure at night, illuminating

leaf after leaf and luminous
bug after bug —

I don't know the names of the
constellations overhead all these
fifty-three years and have to
look them up or
make them up: *The Hydrant, Celestial Rollerskate,
Neptune in His Court of Fishy Wives, The
   Indian Wheel* —

I don't know how to bring up my
two children and find myself
exploding or stunned into an
ignorance that recalls to me my
own father —

I don't know whole passages of poetry, often
used as my defense for writing so
    much of it —

I don't know the mysteries of the Sacred Book, although I've
been shown the sparkling path to its door —

nor the lovely motivations of peoples' faces glowing with
  natural light,

although I suspect the heart's behind it,
and behind those hearts
God's Light —

it's all hints and suspicions. Perhaps we know
more than we know we know —

knowledge is the dark underside of a wide eagle's wing
in flight,

it's unutterable but falls in
   rain and sings on
      stones,

it comes from behind a huge
bellowing canvas at the
side of a stage as
big as a canyon, it

unloads its nuggets on our
path,

wings the size of microbes, microbes the size of
entire universes with
thought-processes and
specific articulations —

we all grow on this turning
merry-go-round of hard rock and plywood,
riding statues of old thoughts about to
crumble into nimbler music —

or we do know but can't say it —
we sit in the light the way a
waterfall starts at a
lip of sharp rock and falls
down without willing it
to a pool far below, surrounded by

small deer and intelligent rodents, mosses
catching the splash —

we know what
sunlight slides across our
flat faces, what

moisture gathers
accompanied by
quiet heartbeats.

9

The weight of a saint's footstep across
   crushing ice,
the rate of his fluttering eyelashes and the
   intricate speech of his heartbeats,
the perfect angle of a hornet's nest under the
   eaves, the
number of bats in our Nigerian attic,
the names, among themselves, of the
   praying mantises, green and brown, that

land at our
   sides and
     eye us in that
        curious way,

everywhere water is
trying to drip to the floor.

Of all the things I don't know
the path to myself is the most
   torturous, wrapped
  tight as a mummy, around
     imponderable ciphers,
memories like sad
  Billie Holiday songs, rising up to high notes with
melancholy difficulty.

The history of genealogies both mine and those
   close to me,

the name of that strange papyrus boat that
   got us here,

the shape and moment of the conveyance that will
take us away.

The taste of rainbows and
why they don't appear more often.

Mythology and its soap-opera tangles, its
murder mystery violence and

    tambourine resonance.

Why it is we stand independently and are
self-propelled, between aisles of golden
vegetables and down corridors of
mortal terror, bodies in
    space, calculating, breathing, eyes blinking,
       tongues turning through the
          grooves of speech,

toward what cataclysmic meaning disrobing at the
last minute before the neurological fireworks of
one kind of death or other?

The fall of a sparrow into the
cupped hands of its Creator.

Our bright swoon at last into those
      Hands.

10

What I do know is
the same mind waking up inside my
   head day after day with the same
obsessions and preoccupations,
and I know someone whose
preoccupations are
    everyone else, whose
mind is the mind of the

    daddy-longlegs as well as the
      grieving mother and the
        man whose psyche is in knots,
who wakes up every day to save them from their
    own precipices and
      frightening falls.

I know the same body encasing this mind, with its
time-bound fluctuations, its
    madman's laboratory of chemical
      hankerings and dilapidations,
its heavy-handedness and its
clumsiness while walking, its
    photo-album of physical imprints
      posing for the
        camera of eternity in
          obscurity.

I know the middle of the story, and have
    the Great Idea about the end of it,
the beginning bang and the ending whimper that is
actually a sigh of light in a dazzling
    corkscrew of joy as it
      flies into the
        nets of Elsewhere.

But I don't know if these same eyes
accompany its flight, and whether they'll be
open to the fantastic landscapes whose
gryphons and unicorns watch the
soul's trajectory as it arcs across,

or whether the soul's eyes will be lids-down
to see with greater clarity through the
    river-ripples of transparent atmospheres,

I don't know about that,

but I do know, and this is more
  difficult, a love that
    filters down through the
      trees of our
    living desires, and
has a face that looks out through all our
individual faces with the
same gaze,

incinerates everything before and after it,
  replacing it with a glow warmer than
companionable flesh, cooler than
    thought ever was or could be,

a love

deeper than depths

wider than distance —

vividly present at the writing of this
treatise on *The Impossibility of Ever Knowing*

and *The Impossibility of Ever Not-Knowing* —

what faces us each instant with

nothing less than our first face —

so at the beginning,

the same exact face

at the end.

                                                              7/7-8/11

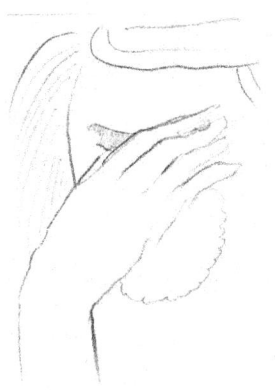

INDEX

After the End of the World   186
Airline Flight 774   80
Annunciatory Angel   77
Another Day   150
Aphorisms   15
Atlantic City Nature Poem   73
Avalanche   82
Back Stairs   167
Baseball Stadium Epiphany   162
Be in a Foreign Country   50
Body-Lock   64
Canyons   17
Certain Poets   18
Death   84
Diversionary Interlude from Puzzle Castle   100
Dust   26
Full Moon   158
Further Aphorisms   86
Getting Dressed   134
I Am a Stubborn Man   163
In Memoriam David Rattray 1937-1993   148
In a World   20
Life and Death   136
Middle of the Night   58
Mockingbird   179
On Being a Guest at Puzzle Castle   89
On Being a Guest at Puzzle Castle II   98
Poem with Two Characters from Shakespeare   22
Point of Departure   30

Puzzlements   173
Reading Oneself   62
Rimbaud in Aden   60
Rock   71
Sleep Twist   110
Sleep and Waking   55
Small Enigmatic Poem   79
Some Poems I Would Like to Write   39
St. Sebastian and St. Jerome's Lion   95
Stripes   66
The Act of Love   177
The Man from Porlock   52
The New Town   175
The Poet Dies   164
The Puzzle   9
The Puzzle Potentized   189
The Puzzle at Present   115
The Wait   168
To be Completely Open   111
Toes   97
Train   105
Unrequited Love   24
Used Bookstore Owner   113
When I Get Transformed into a Woman   45
Whitman's Deathbed   36

ABOUT THE AUTHOR

Born in 1940 in Oakland, California, Daniel Abdal-Hayy Moore had his first book of poems, *Dawn Visions*, published by Lawrence Ferlinghetti of City Lights Books, San Francisco, in 1964, and the second in 1972, *Burnt Heart/Ode to the War Dead*. He created and directed *The Floating Lotus Magic Opera Company* in Berkeley, California in the late 60s, and presented two major productions, *The Walls Are Running Blood*, and *Bliss Apocalypse*. He became a Sufi Muslim in 1970, performed the Hajj in 1972, and lived and traveled throughout Morocco, Spain, Algeria and Nigeria, landing in California and publishing *The Desert is the Only Way Out*, and *Chronicles of Akhira* in the early 80s (Zilzal Press). Residing in Philadelphia since 1990, in 1996 he published *The Ramadan Sonnets* (Jusoor/City Lights), and in 2002, *The Blind Beekeeper* (Jusoor/Syracuse University Press). He has been the major editor for a number of works, including *The Burdah* of Shaykh Busiri, translated by Hamza Yusuf, and the poetry of Palestinian poet, Mahmoud Darwish, translated by Munir Akash. He is also widely published on the worldwide web: *The American Muslim, DeenPort*, and his own website and poetry blog, among others: *www.danielmoorepoetry.com, www.ecstaticxchange.wordpress.com*. He has been poetry editor for *Seasons Journal, Islamica Magazine*, a 2010 translation by Munir Akash of *State of Siege*, by Mahmoud Darwish (Syracuse University Press), and *The Prayer of the Oppressed*, by Imam Muhammad Nasir al-Dar'i, translated by Hamza Yusuf. In 2011 he was a winner of the Nazim Hikmet Prize for Poetry. *The Ecstatic Exchange Series* is bringing out the extensive body of his works of poetry (a complete list of published works on page 2).

POETIC WORKS by Daniel Abdal-Hayy Moore
Published and Unpublished

Dawn Visions (published by City Lights, 1964)
Burnt Heart/Ode to the War Dead (published by City Lights, 1972)
This Body of Black Light Gone Through the Diamond (printed by Fred Stone, Cambridge, Mass, 1965)
On The Streets at Night Alone (1965?)
All Hail the Surgical Lamp (1967)
States of Amazement (1970)

Abdallah Jones and the Disappearing-Dust Caper (published by The Ecstatic Exchange/Crescent Series, 2006)
'Ala ud-Deen and the Magic Lamp
The Chronicles of Akhira (1981) (published by Zilzal Press with Typoglyphs by Karl Kempton, 1986; published in Sparrow on the Prophet's Tomb by The Ecstatic Exchange, 2009)
Mouloud (1984) (A Zilzal Press chapbook, 1995; published in Sparrow on the Prophet's Tomb by The Ecstatic Exchange, 2009)
Man is the Crown of Creation (1984)
The Look of the Lion (The Parabolas of Sight) (1984)
The Desert is the Only Way Out (completed 4/21/84) (Zilzal Press chapbook, 1985)
Atomic Dance (1984) (am here books, 1988)
Outlandish Tales (1984)
Awake as Never Before (12/26/84) (Zilzal Press chapbook, 1993)
Glorious Intervals (1/1/85) (Zilzal Press chapbook, ?)
Long Days on Earth/Book I (1/28 – 8/30/85)
Long Days on Earth/Book II (Hayy Ibn Yaqzan)
Long Days on Earth/Book III (1/22/86)
Long Days on Earth/Book IV (1986)
The Ramadan Sonnets (Long Days on Earth/Book V) (5/9 – 6/11/86) (published by Jusoor/City Lights Books, 1996) (republished as Ramadan Sonnets by The Ecstatic Exchange, 2005)
Long Days on Earth/Book VI (6-8/30/86)
Holograms (9/4/86 – 3/26/87)
History of the World (The Epic of Man's Survival) (4/7 – 6/18/87)
Exploratory Odes (6/25 – 10/18/87)
The Man at the End of the World (11/11 – 12/10/87)

The Perfect Orchestra (3/30 – 7/25/88)(published by The Ecstatic Exchange, 2009)
Fed from Underground Springs (7/30 – 11/23/88)
Ideas of the Heart (11/27/88 – 5/5/89)
New Poems (scattered poems, out of series, from 3/24 – 8/9/89)
Facing Mecca (5/16 – 11/11/89)
A Maddening Disregard for the Passage of Time (11/17/89 – 5/20/90) (published by The Ecstatic Exchange, 2009)
The Heart Falls in Love with Visions of Perfection (6/15/90 – 6/2/91)
Like When You Wave at a Train and the Train Hoots Back at You (Farid's Book) (6/11 – 7/26/91) (published by The Ecstatic Exchange, 2008)
Orpheus Meets Morpheus (8/1/91– 3/14/92)
The Puzzle (3/21/92 – 8/17/93)(published by The Ecstatic Exchange, 2011)
The Greater Vehicle (10/17/93 – 4/30/94)
A Hundred Little 3-D Pictures (5/14/94 – 9/11/95)
The Angel Broadcast (9/29 – 12/17/95)
Mecca/Medina Time-Warp (12/19/95 – 1/6/96) (published as a Zilzal Press chapbook, 1996)(published in Sparrow on the Prophet's Tomb, 2009)
Miracle Songs for the Millennium (1/20 – 10/16/96)
The Blind Beekeeper (11/15/96 – 5/30/97) (published 2002 by Jusoor/Syracuse University Press)
Chants for the Beauty Feast (6/3 – 10/28/97)(published by The Ecstatic Exchange, 2011
You Open a Door and it's a Starry Night (10/29/97 – 5/23/98) (published by The Ecstatic Exchange, 2009)
Salt Prayers (5/29 – 10/24/98) (published by The Ecstatic Exchange, 2005)
Some (10/25/98 – 4/25/99)
Flight to Egypt (5/1 – 5/16/99)
I Imagine a Lion (5/21 – 11/15/99) (published by The Ecstatic Exchange, 2006)
Millennial Prognostications (11/25/99 – 2/2/2000) (published by the Ecstatic Exchange, 2009)
Shaking the Quicksilver Pool (2/4 – 10/8/2000) (published by The Ecstatic Exchange, 2009)
Blood Songs (10/9/2000 – 4/3/2001)
The Music Space (4/10 – 9/16/2001) (published by The Ecstatic Exchange, 2007)
Where Death Goes (9/20/2001 – 5/1/2002) (published by The Ecstatic Exchange, 2009)

The Flame of Transformation Turns to Light (99 Ghazals Written in English) (5/14 – 8/21/2002) (published by The Ecstatic Exchange, 2007)
Through Rose-Colored Glasses (7/22/2002 – 1/15/2003) (published by The Ecstatic Exchange, 2007)
Psalms for the Broken-Hearted (1/22 – 5/25/2003) (published by The Ecstatic Exchange, 2006)
Hoopoe's Argument (5/27 – 9/18/03)
Love is a Letter Burning in a High Wind (9/21 – 11/6/2003) (published by The Ecstatic Exchange, 2006)
Laughing Buddha/Weeping Sufi (11/7/2003 – 1/10/2004) (published by The Ecstatic Exchange, 2005)
Mars and Beyond (1/20 – 3/29/2004) (published by The Ecstatic Exchange, 2005)
Underwater Galaxies (4/5 – 7/21/2004) (published by The Ecstatic Exchange, 2007)
Cooked Oranges (7/23/2004 – 1/24/2005 (published by The Ecstatic Exchange, 2007)
Holiday from the Perfect Crime (1/25 – 6/11/2005)(published by The Ecstatic Exchange, 2011)
Stories Too Fiery to Sing Too Watery to Whisper (6/13 – 10/24/2005)
Coattails of the Saint (10/26/2005 – 5/10/2006) (published by The Ecstatic Exchange, 2006)
In the Realm of Neither (5/14/2006 – 11/12/06) (published by The Ecstatic Exchange, 2008)
Invention of the Wheel (11/13/06 – 6/10/07)(published by The Ecstatic Exchange, 2010)
The Sound of Geese Over the House (6/15 – 11/4/07)
The Fire Eater's Lunchbreak (11/11/07 – 5/19/2008) (published by The Ecstatic Exchange, 2008)
Sparks Off the Main Strike (5/24/2008 – 1/10/2009)(published by The Ecstatic Exchange, 2010)
Stretched Out on Amethysts (1/13 – 9/17/2009)(published by The Ecstatic Exchange, 2010)
The Throne Perpendicular to All that is Horizontal (9/18/09 – 1/25/10)
In Constant Incandescence (2/10 – 8/13/10) (published by The Ecstatic Exchange, 2011)
The Caged Bear Spies the Angel (8/30/10 – 3/6/11)(published by The Ecstatic Exchange, 2010)
This Light Slants Upward (3/7/11 --)

www.ingramcontent.com/pod-product-compliance
Lightning Source LLC
Chambersburg PA
CBHW031627160426
43196CB00006B/307